D1032523

THE ★ ★ ★
WAR ★ ★
CHILD'S ★
CHILDREN

The Story of the Third Regiment,
Arkansas Cavalry, Confederate States Army

by

MAJ. CALVIN L. COLLIER

1965

Also by

CALVIN L. COLLIER:

    THEY'LL DO TO TIE TO

    (Third Arkansas Infantry Regiment, C.S.A.)

    FIRST IN — LAST OUT

    (Capitol Guards, Arkansas Brigade, C.S.A.)

Book Design by
C. ARMITAGE HARPER
Printed in U.S.A.

Maj. Calvin L. Collier

5324 Sherwood Road

Little Rock, Arkansas

The story of the

Third Regiment, Arkansas Cavalry

C. S. A.

To four daughters

who, like me,

loved the service

"THE WAR CHILD'S CHILDREN"

ACKNOWLEDGEMENTS

To produce a work of this type and scope requires the assistance and interest of many persons and organizations. Within this limited space I am pleased to cite some of these places and people whose guidance and help made possible the complicated collection and compilation of the records of the Third Arkansas Cavalry, CSA. Through the generosity of Mr. J. N. Heiskell, Publisher of the Arkansas Gazette, the records of the Third Arkansas were made available to me at the National Archives in Washington D. C. My special thanks to him for his interest in preserving the history of the Confederate Soldiers. To my good friend and confidant, Judge Neill Bohlinger, my thanks for his interest and the use of his vast store of knowledge of the Confederate Soldier and his war.

To Dr. John L. Ferguson and his excellent staff at the Arkansas History Commission, my thanks for their time and patience in helping to research their excellent collection of Confederate records.

Finally, to my wife Jonny, I owe a special debt of gratitude for her unending patience, continuous encouragement, and many hours of typographical and editorial assistance.

Contents

ILLUSTRATIONS

MAPS

Chapter I

"They came out of the wilds of Arkansas and Texas and were the roughest lot of humanity I ever saw. They rode like they were part of the horse and feared nothing on this earth, either human or animal. When not fighting the Yankees, they were fighting each other. They swore most fearfully and drank like demons. Despite their roughness of character with their six-shooters in close combat, they were a formidable Instrument of War."

These words of faint praise from a Tennessee Cavalryman aptly described both the appearance and attitude of the Third Regiment of Arkansas Cavalry, Confederate States Army. Most of them had no particular political beliefs that would have led them to war, nor did they have any particular brief against the enemy. They were, for the most part, rough and hardy pioneer types of western Arkansas whose knowledge of politics was limited to a case hardened belief in self-determination. To them the issue that set off the bloodiest war in history was as simple as life itself. They had elected a legislature that had voted to secede from the Union and establish a free nation of their own. This wish was now being frustrated by Abraham Lincoln who was in the process of applying force to override their wishes. It was as simple as that and nothing more. The average volunteer from Arkansas would say, (as many did), that they had joined the Union voluntarily; and, therefore, they should be able to leave it voluntarily. On this simple premise he was perfectly willing to lay his life on the block.

This attitude carried them to the recruiting bureaus in droves. The City of Little Rock was a seething madhouse of

Major General Joseph Wheeler
"THE WAR CHILD"

military activity. The Federal Arsenal had been seized and the garrison driven from the state. On May 6, 1861 Arkansas seceded from the Union and joined the fledgling Confederacy. As fast as the loosely knit military units could be formed, they were sent off to the border of divided and uncertain Missouri. The military planners for Governor Rector saw Missouri as the route of Federal invasion and thus the lion's share of men and material were forwarded to that area. One of the first units to pitch camp in upper Arkansas was the First Regiment, Arkansas Mounted Volunteers.

Somewhere in the swirling confusion of war preparations in Little Rock, Colonel Solon Borland, Aide to Governor Rector, had received permission to raise a regiment of mounted troops for state service. This work was accomplished on June 10, 1861 when eight companies of horsemen were mustered in on the Arsenal grounds. The rush to get to the Missouri border was so pressing that the needed two companies were left to future recruiting, and Borland left Little Rock with the eight companies already at hand. In late June, these raw soldiers were encamped on the Current River north of Pocahontas in Randolph County.

On July 29th the regiment was officially mustered into the Confederate service as the First Regiment, Arkansas Mounted Volunteers. The original staff was comprised of Solan Borland, Colonel, Commanding; James M. Gee, Lieutenant Colonel; D. F. Shall, Major; and Nathaniel D. Holmes, Adjutant.
They had brought with them from the hills some beautiful examples of horseflesh. Most of the animals were superb in blood and spirit. Even the poorest of these men loved the chase and following a pack of Walker hounds on a bright moonlight night was the supreme joy of life. They were natural horsemen, as much at home over a high post and rail fence as they were going at a trot. Most were masters in the use of both the rifle and the pistol. Tearing at full speed past a row of fence posts on which pumpkins were placed, exploding them with deadly accuracy with a six-shooter, was a daily demonstration in the camps. Those who did not have the somewhat rare six-shooter armed themselves with double-barrel 12 gauge shotguns, or with their favorite hunting rifle or smooth bore brought from home. Some carried two six-shooters and a shotgun. Few had or wanted to have a sabre. This weapon was generally held in contempt by the average enlisted Confederate cavalryman. His idea of close combat was

to ride full tilt into the enemy and blast into them with a double load of buckshot at point-blank range, then wade in with a six-shooter. This peculiarity of tactics was to spell the difference on many a field of mounted combat in the years to come. The Federal cavalryman's reliance on the rather useless sabre, especially when matched against a pair of repeating pistols, cost many of them their lives in the myriad of running fights in the Civil War. Born to the saddle; inured to weather and hardship; expert with firearms; and thoroughly motivated, the Confederate horseman had a decided edge on his Yankee opponent on every field where the odds were anywhere near equal.

As the fratricidal conflict began to gain momentum and shake down into a semblance of breadth and scope in the summer of '61, the Mounted Volunteers entered on active service. Colonel Borland was subordinated to Brigadier William J. Hardee, newly arrived from Mississippi, and assigned to the forward patrols into southern Missouri. Hardee's Headquarters were at Pocahontas where his command consisted of a brigade of Arkansas infantry and a smattering of Missouri troops.

The summer wore into fall with nothing to break the monotony of patroling except personal conflict. The muster rolls covering the summer months reflect three entries indicating that three men were killed as a result of "personal encounter" or "died as a result of personal disagreement." There are many men today who totally disagree with the Southerner's keen belief in integrity and honor in those days. It may have been somewhat destructive in its result, but it made a man mighty careful what he said about another.

The long, inactive spell of good weather in north Arkansas was a boon to the green troops in Hardee's command. Both officers and men learned the rudiments of soldiering. The latest manual on cavalry tactics was studied, and its teachings put in practice hour after hour on the open fields. Colonel Phillip St. George Cook, now a Federal General and father-in-law to Confederate General J. E. B. Stuart, had written the defintive manual on cavalry drill just prior to the outbreak of war and now his enemies were putting it to good use. By late summer the regiment could perform all the intricate maneuvers in the book with precision skill.

In early September, Lieutenant Colonel Gee resigned his post and returned to Little Rock to raise his own regiment and Benjamin F. Danly was appointed in his stead. On September

21st General Hardee and his entire infantry force left Arkansas bound for Kentucky and the army of General Albert Sidney Johnston. The First Arkansas Mounted Volunteers and a few badly organized Missourians were left to watch the vast expanse of country along the border. At this time too, Company "E" was detached from the First and assigned to the Second Arkansas Cavalry east of the Mississippi. They were not to return until January, 1863.

The war west of the Mississippi had gotten underway in a most haphazard fashion. While the Arkansas Cavalrymen whiled away their time at Pitman's Ferry drinking hard liquor and shooting each other, their brethren in Missouri were gathering for the fray. The state was split wide open. Governor Claiborne Jackson was a staunch southerner and was exerting every effort to take Missouri into the Confederacy. He was frustrated by a solid slate of Unionists led by Frances P. Blair, a Republican, and Sterling Price, a Conservative. The result of the State Convention was a down-the-line slate against secession. Jackson then made an effort to take the Federal arsenal at St. Louis but, as in the convention, he was thwarted by Blair and Nathaniel Lyon, Commander of the arsenal. Captain Lyon then captured the Confederate oriented militia camp, an action which resulted in a regiment of nervous Germans firing into a crowd of civilians killing several women and children. This act of violence drove Sterling Price into the Confederate camp where he accepted command of the Missouri Army from Governor Jackson.

The lines were now drawn and the State exploded into action. Price gathered his forces with the skill of a veteran and retreated toward the northwest corner of Arkansas where he could link up with General Ben McCullough's small force of Arkansans and Texans and General N. B. Pierce's Arkansas Brigade. Lyon, now a Brigadier General, began feverish preparations to complete the subjugation of the State. In early August Price, with Pierce and McCullough, advanced on Lyon at Springfield. At this point General Hardee was requested to move into Missouri with his force from Pitman's Ferry and move to the aid of Price. Hardee flatly refused. On August 10th two of the greenest armies ever sent to the field collided at Oak Hills by Wilson's Creek in Missouri and killed each other with fanatic zeal. In Price's small army, his chief of ordnance couldn't tell a Howitzer from a three-inch rifle and, in fact, admitted that he had never seen a musket cartridge in his life. His men knew nothing of drill or soldiering and were armed with every conceivable type of firearm in existence. The officers were identified by bits of flannel cloth pinned to their sleeves. Still, at Oak Hills they fought a bloody little battle with the steadiness of professional soldiers tried in combat.

Early in the fight, General Lyon was killed and in a matter of a few hours the Confederates were masters of the field. The victory proved nothing since both sides remained in relatively the same strategic and tactical position. The action did accomplish one thing—it made good soldiers of many junior officers of both sides. The roster of the Majors and Captains at Oak Hills reads like a Who's Who of top-flight General Officers at the close of the Civil War.

On September 20th the city of Lexington surrendered to Price after a bloody three day seige while Hardee at Pitman's Ferry was assembling his troops for the Kentucky move, an act that left Sterling Price holding the bag.

While warfare raged a scant hundred miles away, the First Arkansas Mounted Volunteers continued to sit it out. Many died of exposure and measles and many others were discharged as overage or infirm. A miserable Christmas was spent in camp. On January 10th they received a new General Officer Commanding in the person of Earl Van Dorn, an energetic West Pointer. Van Dorn was a first class professional soldier and lost no time in bringing order out of chaos in the camps. At this time, too, the Confederate War Department sorted out the innumerable duplication of regimental numbers. There was already in existence a First Arkansas Mounted Rifles then on duty with Price in northwest Arkansas. Thus the First Arkansas Mounted Volunteers became, officially, the Third Arkansas Cavalry, Confederate States Army, a name that was to become a legend in the mounted arm of the Army of Tennessee.

In February, 1862 Van Dorn departed Pocahontas for Fort Smith where he intended to assume command of both Price and McCullough and precipitate action to clear Arkansas of Federals. General Van Dorn got the action he wanted, but he didn't get the victory he sought. In early March, with Price and McCullough now working together under Van Dorn's leadership, the Confederates assailed the Federals under General Samuel Curtis at Pea Ridge in northwest Arkansas. A sanguinary two-day battle raged over the hills ending with the death of McCullough and Confederate defeat. Van Dorn's beaten army retreated southward to Van Buren leaving Curtis in full control of nearly half the state.

Meanwhile, east of the Mississippi, larger things were afoot. General Ulysses S. Grant had captured Forts Henry and Donelson and driven the Confederates from Kentucky. By early April the Confederate Army under Albert Sidney Johnston had concentrated at Corinth in Mississippi while Grant had put his enormous army ashore at Pittsburg Landing in Tennessee, a scant twenty miles away. It was at the latter place that General Johnston elected to make his attack. The outcome of this decision was the great Battle of Shiloh in which Johnston lost the battle and his life. Just prior to the debacle at Shiloh, Confederate General P. G. T. Beauregard ordered all the scattered armies of the Western Confederacy to converge at or near Corinth to offset the heavy losses expected in Tennessee. This order was promptly obeyed by General Van Dorn.

The town of Des Arc on the White River of Arkansas was designated as the collecting point for the Arkansas Armies where convoys of steamboats would transport them to Mississippi. The Third Arkansas Cavalry left the camps on Current River and rode southward through Pocahontas, Jacksonport and Augusta arriving at Des Arc on April 16th. Here they received the unkindest cut of all. General Van Dorn, convinced that infantry and not cavalry was needed beyond the Mississippi, set about dismounting all the horsemen in his command. As every Company Commander so carefully wrote into the muster roll records— "this company was dismounted at Des Arc under the promise that the men should be in a short time remounted and that while they were dismounted they should receive all the privileges and emoluments of regular cavalrymen—." They were to learn that a promise made under peaceful circumstances was hard to keep under combat conditions. The horses were sent to Drew County under charge of one lieutenant, one sergeant and five privates and the Third Arkansas Cavalry (dismounted) was on its way to Mississippi.

On May 1, 1862 Van Dorn's Army under direct command of Sterling Price arrived in the camps at Corinth. They were immediately put into line and were involved in the minor skirmishing at Farmington where the Federals under General Halleck were creeping slowly forward toward Corinth. Here for the first time, the Third Arkansas heard shots really fired in anger.

With the passage of the Conscript Act by the Confederate Government, all armies in the field were ordered to reorganize into regular units, thereby eliminating the provisional status of most of the units. Price issued Special Order No. 98 on May 25th instructing the units of his command to hold elections and re-muster the troops into the regular service. In addition, Lieutenant Colonel John L. Williamson's Battalion of Arkansas Infantry was amalgamated with the Third Cavalry to make up the shortage of three companies needed to make a full regiment. These former infantrymen upon final reorganization became companies "E," "I" and "K" of the Third Cavalry. Previous efforts by the regiment to satisfactorily select their officers is reflected in a letter found in the Official Records addressed to General Price. As noted in the muster rolls, it is evident that the officers in command at the time of reorganization did not meet the approval of any of the rank and file. The entire staff of officers who originally raised the regiment were defeated and transferred from the organization. The aforementioned letter reads as follows:

> Headquarters Third Brigade
> Jones' Division Army of the West
> May 17th, 1862

> General;
> Herewith enclosed is the return of elections for field and company officers in the 3rd Arkansas Cavalry—on the 16th and 17th inst.
> The reorganization of that regiment as held on the 10th inst., a return of which was forwarded to your HD Qrs—was imperfect and unsatisfactory —because of the refusal of many of the men and several entire companies to enter into it—the communication of Lt. Col. Danley upon this point is herewith forwarded from which you will learn that their present reorganization if endorsed will give entire satisfaction to officers and men. I trust therefore and request that the former returns be withdrawn and those herewith transmitted be substituted in their stead.

> I am Genl very respectfully, etc.
> B. Warren Stone
> Colonel Comdg 3rd Brigade

The final senior officer roster eliminated the entire original group and elected in their stead Captain Samuel G. Earle to Colonel, Captain Anson W. Hobson to Lieutenant Colonel and Captain Marzaime W. Henderson to Major. The final reorganization and muster rolls were approved on May 26th, 1862.

Chapter II

COMMAND AND STAFF

Samuel G. Earle, Colonel
Anson W. Hobson, Lt. Colonel
Marzaime J. Henderson, Major
Armistead Burwell, Lt., Adjutant
John L. McClellan, Capt. Quarter Master
David W. Dodd, Captain, Commissary
Lewis B. Noland, Sgt. Major
William B. Thompson, Quarter Master Sgt.
William H. Priddy, Surgeon
Jacob H. Taylor, Asst. Surgeon

COMPANY "A"

Dallas County

Captain William L. M. Holmes
First Lt. Oliver C. Gray
Second Lt. Robert A. Dedman
Third Lt. John A. Wozencraft

First Sgt. T. A. Atkinson
Second Sgt. P. M. Bridges
Third Sgt. H. G. L. Holmes

First Cpl. R. S. Wiley
Second Cpl. W. B. Thompson
Third Cpl. A. E. Kenneday

PRIVATES

Barlow, J. H.
Barret, P. P.
Bass, B. F.
Bass, J. M.
Benson, S. E.
Bethel, R. A.

Blackwell, W. C.
Brown, N. J.
Bullock, T. C.
Capestro, A. A.
Cochran, R. A.
Crawford, H. B.

Cullen, C.
Darby, T. L.
Demasters, J. J.
Dickens, J. C.
Easterling, H. J.
Edwards, L.
Garlington, J. J.
Garret, O. J.
Green, Thomas
Harrel, J.
Harris, William R.
Harrison, R. W.
Hawkins, W. B.
Higgenbotham, William
Hillman, J. E.
Hillman, S. J.
Holmes, B. H.
Holmes, W. A.
Hunter, J. A.
Johnson, R. P.
Kendrick, J. J. T.
Kenneday, D. G.
Kilpatrick, E.
Langford, G. W.
Lea, Henry

Lowery, Isiah
Matlock, J. G.
McClung, J. A.
McFadden, C.
Moxley, W. H.
Owens, J. M.
Posey, J. W.
Pridgeon, M.
Pruitt, J. M.
Rawlins, C. F.
Rogers, H. W.
Rucks, E.
Sallee, G. W.
Smith, T. R.
Stokes, T. A.
Stubblefield, G. W.
Thomas, J. F.
Thomas, N. D.
Turner, W. G.
Waller, J. A.
Ward, J. F.
Wheeler, J.
Wilson, G. B.
Wright, S. B.
Wright, S. M.

COMPANY "B"

Perry County

Captain William H. Blackwell
First Lt. John F. Lindell
Second Lt. George W. Crawford

First Sgt. A. D. McCullough
Second Sgt. Abraham Edlin
Third Sgt. William Lee

First Cpl. J. H. McCullough
Second Cpl. John Creasey
Third Cpl. Abraham Brandon

PRIVATES

Arnett, J. M.
Bates, J. P.
Bates, L. D.
Bland, John
Brazill, G. W.
Brown, Robert
Bunker, J. C.
Cardon, H. M.
Chiles, P. A.
Cobb, G. J.
Cobb, R. H.
Collins, John

Cornwell, James
Couger, J. N.
Cross, A. H.
Douthet, J. B.
Edlin, G. S.
Ellege, C. B.
Ellege, Issac
Evans, G. W.
Friar, E. R.
Friar, R. M.
Fowlks, G. F.
Gibson, G. W.

Hagan, M. C.
Halbrook, Fendre
Herrald, P. N.
Hill, J. R.
Hubbard, Elisha
Hudson, A. C.
Ivey, G. W.
Ivey, M. L.
Johnson, Joseph
Kennedy, John
King, William
Lamb, N. N.
Marcrum, J. R. T.
Marcrum, W. W.
McCullough, J. A.
McCullough, W. S.
Meyers, Jacob
Mitchell, Issac
Morris, John
Musser, J. G.
Myers, Issac
Neagle, R. A.

Nelson, A. H.
Northern, James
Parker, Issac
Phillips, William
Porter, A. A.
Porter, D.
Ragsdill, Jerimiah
Rankin, R. N.
Scott, W. O.
Sosaman, J. A.
Turner, R. N.
Vanhook, W. D.
Vanhouck, J. G.
Waller, J. W.
Watson, J. C.
Watson, G. W.
Williams, T. C.
Willis, W. G.
Whitford, L. D.
Whitney, F. E.
Yancey, T. A.

COMPANY "C"

Saline County

Captain John D. Logan
First Lt. John Barron
Second Lt. John D. Henslee
Third Lt. J. R. Harvey

First Sgt. S. M. Henderson
Second Sgt. G. W. Hubbert
Third Sgt. T. D. Hockersmith

First Cpl. H. A. Wear
Second Cpl. W. W. Wilson
Third Cpl. M. M. Pelton

PRIVATES

Badgett, W. P.
Barnes, J. A.
Barret, D. H.
Coffield, Patrick
Coppock, C.
Coppock, G. W. R.
Crowson, J. F. Sr.
Crowson, J. F. Jr.
Crowson, R. T.
Couch, Lewis
Dodd, D. W.
Edgin, L. H.
Eddleman, J. A. M.
Flippin, A. B.

Forsythe, J. M.
Garret, O. J.
Goodin, Theo
Goodwin, G.
Grayham, A. J.
Harp, Joshua
Harvey, M. M.
Haynes, C. W.
Henderson, Percivil
Henry, John R.
Hobbs, Gideon
Huffstutler, Aaron
Irons, A. J.
James, William

[11]

Johnson, D. D.
Johnson, Gilman
Johnson, J. H.
Jones, A. J.
Jones, F. M.
Kirkpatrick, D. Y.
Langley, H. B.
Lecroy, A. D.
Lecroy, W. G.
Lecroy, W. T.
Lee, D. C.
Lewis, O. P.
McAdoo, J. A.
McCrory, J. F.
Medlock, J. F.
Medlock, J. H.
Mitchell, Eli
Nabors, J. L.

Nabors, William C.
Needham, H. S.
Needham, William
Osborne, George
Partin, J. J.
Pratt, M. D.
Price, Joseph
Puck, M. M.
Reid, Corrin
Rowland, Alex E.
Scott, W. M.
Stephens, A. M.
Swinford, H. F.
Tinkle, Thaddeus
Ward, Elam D.
Young, Samuel
Young, W. D.

COMPANY "D"

Pulaski County

Captain R. M. King
First Lt. Thomas C. DeCaulp
Second Lt. William J. Bass

First Sgt. Thomas Brookins
Second Sgt. James Smith
Third Sgt. John Parker

First Cpl. D. M. Starbuck
Second Cpl. George Heckler
Third Cpl. G. W. Moreland

PRIVATES

Atkins, Andrew
Atkins, Harrison
Austin, Bartlett
Beane, James
Bohrer, Charles
Bridges, A. N. M. B.
Burlison, J. C.
Burns, W. D.
Bylema, W. R.
Campbell, G. W.
Cappo, John
Carey, T. B.
Chandler, D. A.
Chenault, J. M.
Chesney, Oliver
Condit, J. S. M.
Cox, J. G.
Drain, James
Dunn, E. S.
Dupee, W. D.

Field, H. D.
Fiero, Akim
Fletcher, Martin
Fox, William
Henderson, J. P.
Holcomb, John
James, Samuel
Kline, Fred
Klingelheoffer, G.
Lindsey, Enos
Marguett, John
McNabb, Mahlen
Moore, W. H.
Ogelsby, Robert
Paine, Thomas
Peavyhouse, M. J. G.
Reading, Samuel
Rylan, William R.
Rupell, R. R.
Scott, T. C.

Shipe, Jackson
Shuford, E. D.
Smith, J. M. B.
Spikes, J. L.
Spikes, W. W.
Stewart, V. A.

Taylor, Peter
Thomas, W. H.
Vandeven, Noah
Waits, F. M.
White, A. B.
Winchester, J. S.

1st COMPANY "E"

Detached, Sept. 1861, returned Jan., 1863
Pulaski County

Captain A. B. Duke
1st Lt. Joseph T. Cole
2nd Lt. E. P. Clingman

1st Sgt. Will D. Hinson
2nd Sgt. William Fullwood
3rd Sgt. Ezekial Church
4th Sgt. T . Organ Sr.

1st Cpl. W. N. Owen
2nd Cpl. H. D. Heard
3rd Cpl. E. B. Tollison
4th Cpl. N. B. Petty

PRIVATES

Berry, S. A.
Beasley, Thomas
Bell, Samuel
Burrow, M. P.
Bogart, S. H.
Bryant, William
Canada, W. J.
Carter, D. H.
Chambers, George
Clarnpit, W. S.
Cole, John A.
Coney, J. N.
Cowan, James
Crawford, S. S.
Damon, G. W.
Davis, E. G.
Davis, O. C.
Denning, John
Evans, John
Garland, S. G.
Glasgow, A. H.
Glaze, M. J.
Graves, Thomas
Harris, H. S.
Hemphill, R. T.
Hood, W. T.
Ivey, H. T.
Jowers, E. G.
Kirksey, E. P.

Langston, Asa
Lee, W. P.
Lenox, John P.
Marr, G.
Martin, John D.
McClain, Archie
McGehee, Joseph
McMakin, P. C.
Moore, R. N. N.
Morgan, McGibberley
Moody, Joseph
Moss, F. M.
Mullins, Jasper
Neeley, D.
Oliver, J. A.
O'Lear, A. A.
Organ, John N.
Pilkington, Dan
Pritchard, William
Quest, Robert
Radikar, C. E.
Rogers, W. S.
Scott, G. W.
Scott, R. L.
Spain, Henery De
Spain, Clenden De
Stowker, Durkin
Sydnor, W. A.
Thompson, G. W.

Tycer, W. M.
Walbrink, Frank
Wallace, R. N.
Warren, C. P.

West, George H.
Wooten, R. T.
Wright, Jasper

2nd COMPANY "E"

Pope County

Captain James L. Adams
1st Lt. Dan C. Brown
2nd Lt. John M. Strayhorn
3rd Lt. James D. Barret

1st Sgt. William R. Hoggins
2nd Sgt. William C. Wheeler
3rd Sgt. Jonathan Mearshaw

1st Cpl. Richard Cobb
2nd Cpl. Lee Mahan
3rd Cpl. Henery D. Powers
4th Cpl. Richard Ward

PRIVATES

Ada, Edmond
Ashworth, Benjamin
Barnes, John R.
Barron, Jason
Bassett, Alsey
Battenfield, James M.
Bonds, George
Carter, Berry H.
Chambers, W. H.
Chaso, John
Church, L.
Cobb, Ambrose
Conley, R. W.
Daniels, Wiley E.
Esters, Jasper
Guest, J. W.
Guest, Thomas
Hagood, Aloise
Henson, Jacob
Hinchey, D. K. P.
Jones, John
Kent, John G.
Lee, Thomas
Moore, Thomas A.

Morrow, John
Morton, John W.
Neeley, William G.
Owens, Alford I.
Owens, William P.
Parrish, James
Powers, Hugh R.
Ramsey, W. H.
Rankins, W. K.
Ross, William F.
Sinclair, Albert
Sinclair, Thomas
Smith, Thomas
Smith, Sam
Stansell, W. A.
Tyler, Calvin
Tyler, Edwin
Wells, John C.
Williamson, George
Williamson, H. W.
Williamson, James F.
Williamson, John L.
Wood, Thomas A.

COMPANY "F"

Hot Spring County

Captain Steven Jester
1st Lt. William H. Parks
2nd Lt. John Sumpter
3rd Lt. John Bartholomew

1st Sgt. David F. Parker	1st Cpl. John M. L. McClellan
2nd Sgt. John W. Dyer	2nd Cpl. Adam Sharp
3rd Sgt. W. H. Rigsby	3rd Cpl. William M. Grant
	4th Cpl. John Thomas

PRIVATES

Adams, J. S.
Adams, J. Q.
Addy, Josiah
Attaway, William
Banford, Joseph
Barker, Joseph
Bassett, Henry
Bartholomew, J. N.
Bean, Calloway
Blake, W. D.
Brock, Z.
Brooks, William
Brown, Hayman
Burke, Michael
Burkes, George
Burkes, James
Buster, George
Byers, Nicholas
Byers, Phillip
Campbell, S. P.
Casteel, John H.
Chamberlin, John
Chamberlin, William
Christian, J. E.
Compton, Gideon
Daniels, William
Davis, John
Davis, William
Davaney, Manuel
Dyer, Demetrious
Dyer, William
Evans, Jesse
Finey, William
Flewellen, William
Floyd, James F.
Gentry, Samuel
Gardenhire, Jackson

Gardenhire, James
Garner, William
Garwood, William
Gollaher, David
Gollaher, Madison
Green, Jasper
Green, Thomas
Harrison, Joseph
Hayes, Washington
Haupt, Henry
Henderson, Percival
Hunnicutt, E. N.
Hunnicutt, George
Hutchingson, John
Hutchingson, Thomas
Irons, Jonathan
Jester, John
Jones, David
Kempner, Jacob
Kline, Lewis
Langford, D. N. F.
Langley, John
Magby, James
Magby, Silas
Martin, Jasper
McDaniel, J. A.
McDaniel, Joseph
McDaniel, Martin
McKinley, Thomas A.
McLenan, Bursel
McLenan, John
Newton, John B.
Nobles, Nathaniel
Nobles, Randall
Norman, Asberry
Oates, Thomas
Owens, A. B.

[15]

Pollack, Myer
Ray, Isaac
Rice, Edwin
Rigsby, Ben
Rigsby, George
Rigsby, James
Ripetto, Joseph
Sammons, John
Sammons, Robert
Sammons, S. A.
Scruggs, Richard

Skieff, Terry
Sumpter, John
Tillery, William
Vansickel, Miles
Vansickel, William
Walter, W. B.
Warford, James
Warford, Wilson
White, James
White, T. N.
Wright, John

COMPANY "G"

Ouachita County

Captain George W. Winburne
1st Lt. Jeremiah E. Dumas
2nd Lt. David T. Henry
3rd Lt. James P. Roland

1st Sgt. Robert Brazil
2nd Sgt. William Kennaday
3rd Sgt. Robert H. Joiner

1st Cpl. Thomas D. Arnold
2nd Cpl. N. P. Gordon
3rd Cpl. William P. Blackwell

PRIVATES

Barnett, James
Black, Cicero S.
Blumenthal, Samuel
Bridges, A. J.
Bridges, William
Brown, William
Cartrekl, John W.
Childers, Alberry
Coleman, John
Day, Thomas
Dumas, I. A.
Dumas, Frances
Earle, F. W.
Fletcher, George W.
Frazier, George W.
Higgins, Stephen F.
Howard, W. B.
Jones, William
Junial, J. W.
Malier, David G.
Mays, David M.
McLinden, Charles B.
Mitchell, James
Minor, John C.
Moore, James M.
Mosley, James

Moss, Albert A.
Newberry, John H.
Nutt, Sampson
Nutt, William
Nutt, William M.
Oglesby, James
Padgett, Alexander
Parham, Charles
Parham, Robert
Patterson, Samuel
Perkins, H. H.
Pilcher, George
Posey, B. T.
Riggs, James
Riggs, William
Roland, James
Ross, Frank
Stephenson, William
Thomas, Lindsay P.
Thompson, David
Thompson, John
Thompson, Joseph
Toms, Edward H.
Wages, Morgan J.
Williams, William D.
Winburne, Finch

COMPANY "H"

Ouachita County

Captain Alonzo Montgomery
First Lt. Henry C. Cleaver
Second Lt. John L. Harris
Third Lt. Charles Leake

First Sgt. B. M. Scott
Second Sgt. E. E. Pace
Third Sgt. A. O. Scott

First Cpl. David Fritch
Second Cpl. R. H. Baber
Third Col. John T. Downs

PRIVATES

Atkins, Eonidas
Atkins, B. T.
Atkins, W. H.
Aven, A. L.
Ayers, Jeff W.
Barr, James
Battle, T. V.
Bowling, David
Bradshaw, Charles
Brewer, William
Browning, John
Brown, G. W.
Buck, G. W.
Carroll, J. P.
Chambliss, J. M.
Christopher, J. N.
Cook, J. T.
Cranford, H. C.
Danley, John
Deed, Bryant
Dixon, Jesse
Edwards, W. W.
Farmington, W. D.
Furr, J. M.
Grayson, F. M.
Grayson, Thomas
Green, Alexander
Green, Daniel
Green, J. M.
Green, Parnell
Haigwood, B. B.
Harrington, William
Harrist, J. A.
Haltom, E. L.
Haltom, J. D.
Haltom, William
Hinson, J. C.
Hobson, F. A.

Hobson, J. N.
Jordan, J. C. M.
Keifer, S.
Kellam, George
Kelso, B. F.
Kelso, H. A.
Leer, John
Lewis, Hamlin
Lewis, Henry
Lewis, S. P.
Mangrum, J. D.
Marks, T. S.
Martin, R. M.
Massey, J.
McAllister, Newton
McCall, J. A.
McEvers, L. N.
Morrison, John
Orme, L. II.
Owens, James
Owens, Thomas
Owens, W. J.
Patten, J. L.
Patterson, Josiah
Payne, C. C.
Payne, David
Poindexter, William
Rae, Robert
Ratliffe, J. E.
Rice, Robert
Robson, L. Q. C.
Roundtree, B. M.
Roy, Martin E.
Scott, Jesse
Scott, William
Smith, W. E.
Thomas, Richard
Traylor, William P.

Vestal, A. A.   Wilson, J. M.
Vestal, G. W.   Wilson, T. D.
Wall, L. H.   Wilson, William
Weaver, H. A.   Williamson, Harvey

COMPANY "I"

Conway County

Captain Marion E. Davis
First Lt. Fountain P. Hervey
Second Lt. Henry N. Atkins
Third Lt. David W. Bizzell

First Sgt. Thomas J. Kelly   First Cpl. John R. H. Hobbs
Second Sgt. Harry May   Second Cpl. William G. Mason
Third Sgt. Robert S. Farrish   Third Cpl. William H. Cobb
Fourth Sgt. John W. Buckner   Fourth Cpl. Henry C. Hargis

PRIVATES

Allen, Jesse E.   Henson, Jacob
Anderson, William A.   Hinson, Edward R.
Bain, Robert A.   Hogins, William N.
Ballard, James K. P.   Jenkins, David L.
Battenfield, Joseph M.   Jones, John J.
Brandon, Edward M.   Jones, Robert C.
Carter, Berry H.   Kelly, Thomas J.
Casey, Ely   Kemp, Richard M.
Chambers, William H.   Knight, William C.
Church, Larkin J.   Lackie, Thomas M.
Clifton, William A.   Mason, William G.
Cobb, Richard D.   McDonald, Julius
Cobb, William   McGowan, William S.
Cox, James B.   Mount, Robert W.
Davis, James E.   Neeley, William
Dowell, John   Powell, John W.
Forbus, John   Plunkett, Abraham
Forbus, Stephen   Plunket, Lewis D.
Fuller, Thomas   Ramsey, William H.
Garrison, Andrew   Roberts, Elsberry
Garrison, Aĩen W.   Roberts, James H.
Gordon, William C.   Roberts, William T.
Gordon, William T.   Sevier, Henry
Gray, Zack   Sevier, Michael
Green, James S.   Sevier, William
Guest, Thomas   Smith, Samuel
Hale, William N.   Smith, Thomas
Hargis, Harry C.   Sledge, Henry
Harris, Elisha   Steele, Milas W.
Harrison, Craven   Still, James T.
Henry, Ezekial   Stanley, Richard M.

[18]

Straughan, Peter C.
Sutton, William S.
Tapp, Joseph
Thompson, John
Troutt, James C.
Tyler, Calvin
Tyler, Edwin

Vance, Walter J.
Vernon, James
Wheeler, William C.
White, James
Wills, James C.
Wilson, Henry H.
Witt, Alvin

COMPANY "K"

Yell County

Captain W. B. Keeton
First Lt. John M. Cardon
Second Lt. John J. Walker
Third Lt. W. V. Sutherland

First Sgt. Thomas J. Bates
Second Sgt. Berry Lee
Third Sgt. John P. Bata
Fourth Sgt. Charles Wamsee

First Cpl. William Wilburn
Second Cpl. L. D. Bata
Third Cpl. George Gibson
Fourth Cpl. John Moore

PRIVATES

Alexander, John M.
Arnett, John M.
Baker, B. W.
Baker, E. C.
Barnett, John
Brumley, Mathia
Cheek, Thomas
Clounger, William
Cosby, Leander
Costlow, Joseph
Cougar, Jasper
Dawson, Burrel
Dunford, John T.
Flurry, John T.
Flurry, John
Flurry, Henry
Fowlkes, George
Fritch, William W.
Hogan, Matt C.
Hubbard, William E.
Hudson, A. G.
Jordan, Jeremia
Kinney, William
Latham, John
Linbocker, Jonathan
Morgan, George
Nicholson, J. O.

Park, Andy
Parks, David
Patillo, John
Pennel, A. T.
Phillips, J. G.
Phillips, W. N.
Potts, William
Priddy, W. H.
Rigdon, Ephraim
Roberson, Francis M.
Sears, Henry M.
Scarlet, A. P.
Stevens, Berrel
Swammy, Hinson H.
Test, Conrad
Teter, James
Turner, Robert
Vaughan, G. W.
Walker, Albany
Weaver, Hugh C.
Whitford, L. R.
Whitford, W. M.
Whitney, Francis P.
Williams, J. B.
York, Henry
York, Joseph

TEAMSTERS

The Teamsters' roster and pay roll were maintained as a separate unit from the usual military muster rolls. The Teamsters' mission was to maintain the wagons in serviceable condition and care for the animals used in the supply train. They drove the wagons while the regiment was on the move.

AKIM FIERO, Wagon Master

Buster, George
Garret, A. G.
Hinson, J. C.
Holcomb, John
James, William
Johnson, D. D.
Kennedy, D. G.

Mays, David
McAllister, N.
Owens, Joseph T.
Owens, Thomas
Scruggs, R. M.
Skief, J. W.

INVENTORY

7 six-horse wagons
3 four-horse wagons
1 two-horse wagon

Chapter III

Corinth

General P. G. T. Beauregard brought the broken and bleeding Confederate Army from Shiloh to Corinth. The mighty Albert Sidney Johnston was dead—killed in the early flush of victory at Shiloh—and Beauregard had inherited the beaten command. The Grand Creole's first order was to bring in all the scattered units in grey from Mobile to Little Rock. He was somewhat late in this since the men from Arkansas had already obeyed the earlier summons from Johnston and were enroute by steamboat from Des Arc and would arrive within a week. This accession of 20,000 Arkansans and Missourians was still not enough to match the ponderous force of Federals rapidly approaching a strength of 120,000. Beauregard's one advantage at Corinth was the dilatory movements of General Halleck who was entrenching every yard of ground on his march from Shiloh to confront the Rebels at Corinth. Beauregard had no intention of allowing himself to be besieged by this overwhelming force and was making plans to move south to Tupelo on the Mobile and Ohio Railroad.
On May 29th, after thoroughly confusing Halleck by running empty trains back and forth all night, the Greybacks were long gone. A slow leisurely withdrawal was made despite the best effort of the Federals, and it wasn't until early in June that permanent camp was made in the vicinity of Tupelo. Here General Beauregard took sick leave from the army and left General Braxton Bragg in temporary command. This action provoked the wrath of President Jefferson Davis who held no personal love for Beauregard. He therefore fired one of the best officers in the Confederacy and gave the job permanently to Bragg, an act that was to prove a fatal error.

Maj. Gen. P. G. T. Beauregard

Maj. Gen. Braxton Bragg

General Halleck solved most of the Confederate problems for them shortly after the retreat from Corinth. He scattered the Federal Army over the countryside from middle Tennessee to western Mississippi for the purpose of securing the railroads in preparation for an eventual advance into eastern Tennessee and Chattanooga. Bragg, when apprised of the situation, resolved upon the only brilliant move of his career—an advance into mid-Tennessee and Kentucky. He promptly began preparations for the move. At this point Sterling Price decided to separate himself from the turmoil by pleading a personal case to Jefferson Davis for transfer of his army back to Arkansas and his native Missouri. The eyeball-to-eyeball contest between the President of the Confederacy and General Sterling Price was a masterpiec of vituperation and mutual sarcasm. Price bearded Davis in the capitol building at Richmond and received only bitter recrimination for his pains. He returned to Mississippi with nothing to show for his trip but a badly singed pride.

As soon as Bragg completed his preparations, his army was loaded on the trains and left for Chattanooga. Price was left with his two divisions and orders to prevent Grant from sending troops to reenforce Don Carlos Buel in central Tennessee. Meanwhile, General Van Dorn had been appointed Commander of the Mississippi Department and was at Vicksburg attending to the defense of that place.

No sooner had Bragg arrived at Chattanooga than the hornet's nest began to stir. He had stolen a magnificent march on the Federals and was now far beyond their left flank and moving toward their rear. Grant began shifting troops. The Federal Command was his since General Halleck had been called to Washington as supreme commander of all the armies of the Union. Price promptly petitioned Van Dorn for aid to strike northward between Grant and Buell, divide the two and move into central Tennessee. Van Dorn was now involved in the ill-fated expedition to Baton Rouge under General Breckenridge and could offer no support. In fact, Van Dorn countered by asking Price for aid which "Old Pap" promptly declined. Price then told Van Dorn he was moving in three days with or without his help. Van Dorn, now at Holly Springs, referred the matter to Jefferson Davis and asked for command of both his and Price's force. Davis approved this request without passing his order through Bragg thus committing a double error of judgment.

Price was unaware of this last order as he was marching

steadily forward on the roads to Iuka in northern Mississippi. Price's Army was organized into two divisions. The first under Brigadier General Henry Little and the second under Brigadier General Dabney H. Maurey. Maurey's Division consisted of the Arkansas Brigade under Brigadier General William L. Cabell; Brigadier General John C. Moore's Brigade of mixed Arkansas, Alabama and Texas troops; and Brigadier General C. W. Phifer's Brigade. Phifer's Brigade was made up of the Third Arkansas Cavalry (dismounted) ; Sixth Texas Cavalry (dismounted) ; Ninth Texas Cavalry (dismounted) ; and Colonel Ras Stirman's Battalion of Sharpshooters. On September 14th Price marched into Iuka.

Price did not reckon with the speed with which Grant reacted. The Federal Commander lost not a moment. General E. O. C. Ord and General Rosecrans were on their way to intercept Price within a day after his arrival at Iuka. Ord moving from Burnsville and Rosecrans moving from Jacinto put the pincers on the town long before daylight on the 19th. Leaving Maury's Division to watch and intercept Ord, Price led Little's Division south of the town to assail the oncoming Rosecrans. Thus was precipitated the nasty little battle of Iuka. Though only one Confederate Division and two Federal Divisions were involved, the fight was a desperate bloody contest. Price captured nine guns and drove the Federals from the field. This little victory went for naught when Van Dorn, who had just received orders giving him command over Price and his Army of the West, ordered Price to retreat immediately in the direction of Baldwyn. This movement was executed without loss or difficulty. The Third Arkansas and Maury's Division did not fight at Iuka, but sat in watch over Ord and listened to the roar of Price's battle scarce five miles away. Their day was yet to come.

With the amalgamation of Price's Army with General Mansfield Lovell's Division, Van Dorn's force at Ripley was 22,000 men. Price had marched from Baldwyn to Ripley on the 26th in obedience to Van Dorn's order and joined him in that town to discuss the next enterprise. It was an enterprise indeed. Van Dorn proposed to move on Corinth and attack that entrenched camp for the purpose (he said) of preventing Grant from reenforcing Buell in Kentucky. This rash decision was later to be hashed out in a Military Court of Inquiry in which there were hints that Van Dorn was purely on a glory hunting mission. If it was glory he was hunting, he certainly found it on the blood-soaked fields at Corinth. This place was an entrenched camp of the finest type that military engineering could devise and was garrisoned by at least 23,000 first-class fighting men. Nothing daunted, General Earl Van Dorn marched to Corinth.

Through Ruckersville to Jonesboro, northward at that place and on to Pocahontas they tramped and on October 2nd occupied Chewalla. Now Rosecrans knew not only Van Dorn's whereabouts, but his intentions as well. With this intelligence the Federal Commander prepared to receive him. Davies and Hamilton's Divisions posted strong picket lines far out on the west and north fringes of the old Confederate trenches astride the Mobile and Ohio Railroad while the inner lines were manned to the hilt with infantry and artillery.

At daylight on October 3rd, 1862, Van Dorn's advance struck the Federal Brigade under Brigadier General Oliver just east of Chewalla. Oliver fought hard and skillfully. The faint hope of surprising the garrison of Corinth existed only in the mind of Earl Van Dorn. October 3rd was a hot day. Indian Summer struck northern Mississippi that year with the fury of mid-August and the Confederates were without water. By the time Rosecrans' force had been developed astride the Memphis and Charleston Railroad, every canteen in the Rebel Command was dry. Van Dorn formed his line of battle with Lovell's Division to the right of the Chewalla Road; Maury's Division in the center to the left of the Chewalla Road; and Hébert's Division on the left stretching almost to the Mobile and Ohio Railroad. In this position, the attack moved out. The Rebels were surprised at the ferocity with which the Federals fought. General John MacArthur was now in the front with his brigade and was supported by Mower of Stanley's Division. For hours the bloody fighting moved slowly in the direction of Corinth. MacArthur and Mower's troops fought with the greatest tenacity slowing the Rebel advance to a near crawl. When darkness fell Van Dorn was still 600 yards from the main line of resistance and his battle was yet to be fought. His losses had been heavy in a "skirmish" and he was now looking at Corinth over a lace-work of entrenchments, redans, abatis, revetments and rifle pits all bristling with the glint of bayonets. His decision was to stay on the field and carry the town next day—a decision he regretted to the day of his death.

During darkness the Rebels were realigned. Lovell moved up until his left rested on the southside of the Memphis and Charleston Railroad; Maury's Division was placed squarely between the two railroads where their view ahead was one of an ever narrowing gap as the two railroads converged in the outer edge of the town. In addition, Battery Robinett and extensive trenchworks were in their front. General Hébert's Division was placed on the left of Maury astride the Purdy Road and facing Battery Powell. In this position they awaited the dawn.

In the ranks of the Third Arkansas apprehension and doubt of success were rampant. As in many other regiments, several men left the ranks and escaped in the darkness. By brigades Maury's alignment was with General John C. Moore on the right; General C. W. Phifer's next; General William L. Cabell's on the left connecting with the right brigade of Hébert.

At 4:30 a. m. on October 4th Van Dorn's Artillery opened the ball. After an hour of fruitless bombardment the order was passed down the files to move out and strike straight ahead for Corinth. Breaking through the brush, crashing through the abatis and up the swale, the Arkansas men tramped. On topping the high ground it was like stepping into the maw of Hell. From Battery Powell on the left to Battery Robinett in the immediate front, the Federals opened with everything they had. The blast of cannon and roar of rifle fire blended into one earth-shaking rumble and clouds of oily smoke rolled heavenward. The rising screech of the Rebel Yell mingled with the screams of the dying as the ragged horde swept onward. Never on a battlefield so small was the awesome destruction of massed fire-power so magnificently demonstrated. The Confederates were dropping in ever increasing numbers as they advanced. The Yankees in their entrenchments had perfect shooting gallery practice and were pouring it on. The gruesome bravery of the Rebel officers and men in this senseless bloodbath is one of the truly great stories of human conflict. In front of Battery Robinett Colonel William P. Rogers of the Second Texas led three separate assaults on this redan stumbling over his own dead each time. On the third try the works were carried and Rogers was shot dead while standing atop the parapet waving his battleflag and urging on his brave Texans. Colonel S. L. Ross and his Sixth Texas went into Robinett side by side with the Second and the gallant Ross fell within a few feet of Rogers, badly wounded.

Just to the left of the Texans the Third Arkansas men were falling like autumn leaves. By the time the walls of Battery Robinett were breached, Lieutenant John M. Strayhorn was down severely wounded; Lieutenant William H. Parks was shot in the

Maj. Gen. Earl Van Dorn   Maj. Gen. Sterling Price

Confederate slaughter in front of Battery Robinett at Corinth

head; Captain George W. Winburne was down, wounded; Lieutenant J. A. Wozencraft was breathing his last; Captain R. M. King was crippled and soon to die; Lieutenant F. C. DeCaulp was shot through the legs; Captain W. B. Keeton was down, wounded; and Lieutenant H. M. Carden was grieviously injured by shell splinters. In addition to the heavy loss in officers, one hundred enlisted men were to fall on that gory ground. In several companies, every officer, sergeant and corporal was either killed or wounded.

The Federal line finally caved slowly in. To the left of the Third Arkansas, Cabell's Brigade fought their way into the town. The Arkansas men of Cabell actually reached the Tishomingo Hotel and the Town Square. Here the Federals struck back with their reserves and the hand-to-hand fighting became a wild, murderous melee in the streets. Colonel John N. Daly of the Eighteenth Arkansas and Colonel H. P. Johnson of the Twentieth Arkansas were killed in the streets along with half their gallant regiments. On the Confederate left, General Hébert, the Louisiana Creole, replacing the dead Little killed at Iuka, led his men against Battery Powell and the Federal right with the same result as other parts of the Rebel line. His men were simply slaughtered like cattle in a pen. At 1 p. m. even Van Dorn had had enough. The recall was sounded and the bleeding, shattered remnants of his army gathered in the hollows west of Corinth. The Battle of Corinth went down in the pages of history as one of the more foolhardy military efforts ever attempted. The entire campaign was a miserable piece of poor judgment on the part of Van Dorn, but his brave men had inscribed an immortal chapter in the story of American fighting men.

The slaughter at Corinth was part one of Van Dorn's two-part folly. He had neglected to care for the heavy Federal Garrisons in Bolivar and Jackson in Tennessee. These garrisons were at this time coming by forced marches to intercept his escape. Generals Hurlburt and Ord were closing in on the Hatchie River crossings and time was running out. Finally, being apprised of this danger, Van Dorn put his weary army on the march and drove them unmercifully up the roads toward Pocahontas and the Hatchie.

At daylight on the 5th the weary Confederates reached Davis' Bridge on the Hatchie only to find Hurlburt's troops under General Ord blocking the way. Ord immediately assaulted the head of Van Dorn's column. Ord was severely wounded in the first fire, but his men pressed on. The Rebels needed no urging to fight. Their very lives and freedom were at stake and they fought like cornered lions. Every man who could pack his way to the front, loaded and fired as fast as hands could move. A terrible volume of fire was encountered by both sides as a result of crowding on the narrow trails in the dense woods along the river bank. In a matter of minutes in the Third Arkansas, Captain William T. M. Holmes of "A" Company was dead and eleven enlisted men were down to rise no more. Armstrong's Cavalry discovered a ford across a mill dam five miles below the bridge and, undoubtedly, saved the remnant of Van Dorn's Army. At darkness they were over the river and hot-footing it for safety in the sparsely settled country of western Mississippi. Their dead and wounded were left behind at the mercy of the enemy at both Corinth and Hatchie River. Every man knew that he was lucky to get off with his life and was not concerned with those unable to maintain the pace. A panicked military unit is a sickening sight and Van Dorn's Army was fleeing in panic. They were not to halt until safety was reached behind the cavalry at Holly Springs.

In addition to the death or crippling by gunfire at Corinth and Hatchie River, one man fell victim to one of the strange ironies of war. In the panicked retreat from the Hatchie River, the engineers felled trees throughout the night to retard the progress of the pursuit. In the struggling, confused mass of humanity moving forward on the narrow crowded roads, one of these trees fell on Private John Newberry of the Third Arkansas killing him instantly.

At Holly Springs the dismounted Arkansas Cavalrymen toted up the score. At Corinth they had left behind 107 men dead, wounded or captured. At Hatchie River another 11 men and one officer were dead. This grim total of 120 casualties had put fully one-third of the regiment hors-de-combat. Payment for their long days of peace on the Current River in Arkansas had been exacted with a vengeance.

Chapter IV

Cavalrymen at Holly Springs

On arrival with the Army at Tupelo, Colonel Earle had decided to make another effort to have the horses returned and this time through the General Officer Commanding. A letter was prepared and addressed to General Sterling Price, dated 26 August, 1862 at Tupelo, Mississippi.

Genl;

The undersigned officers of the 3rd Regiment Arkansas Cavalry would respectfully represent to you that they were temporarily dismounted at Des Arc Arkansas in the month of April last by order of Genl Earl Van Dorn.

The horses belonging to the Regiment were sent home with the understanding that the Regiment would be remounted. They are still held in readiness and can be procured at short notice.

We respectfully request that we may be allowed to remount and to effect this that authority be given us to send a small detail to procure our horses.

We respectfully represent to you that there is no (mounted) Cavalry regiment from Arkansas in your Army and that this is the oldest Regiment having entered State Service as early as the 7th June 1861.

Genl, we entered the service as cavalry from choice. When called upon to dismount we obeyed the order cheerfully.

To you we now submit our request being conscious that you will do us justice in the premises and assuring you that we will cheerfully submit to your decision.

(SIGNED)

TO MAJ. GENL PRICE
   Cmdg Army of *the* West

Samuel G. Earle
Col Comdg 3rd Ark. Cavalry
M. J. Henderson, Major
Wm. T. M. Holmes, Co. A

G. W. Winburne, Capt. Co. G
W. H. Blackwell, Capt. Co. B
S. W. Crawford, 2nd Lt. Co. B
H. C. Cleaver, 1st Lt. Co. H
J. F. Tindell, Lt. Co. B
W. H. Parks, 1st Lt. Co. F
John H. Bartholomew, Lt. Co. F
Stephen Jester, Captain Co. F
O. C. Gray, 1st Lt. Co. A
R. M. King, Captain Co. D
Thos. C. DeCaulp, 1st Lt. Co. D

W. J. Bass, 3rd Lt. Co. D
J. L. Harris, 2nd Lt. Co. H
R. H. Dedman, 2nd Lt. Co. A
J. A. Wozencraft, 3rd Lt. Co. A
J. D. Logan, Capt., Comdg., Co. C
John Banon, 1st Lt. Co. C
J. D. Henslee, 2nd Lt. Co. C
James R. Harvey, 3rd Lt. Co. C
C. W. Leake, 3rd Lt. Co. H
J. H. Roland, 3rd Lt. Co. G
J. E. Dumas, 1st Lt. Co. G

The first thing that strikes the eye in reading this letter contained in the Official Records is that as time wore on it reads like the roll call of the dead. The letter and request was approved by General Price and forwarded to General Beauregard. Through long, tortuous military channels the letter made its way and was finally approved, but not until the regiment had fought the disastrous battle at Corinth.

The army moved on south to Lumpkin's Mill where winter camp was made. It was here that the regiment's horses were returned from Arkansas arriving in the camps in mid-November. Once again the Third Arkansas was cavalry without the onerous word (dismounted) attached to its name. In addition the Texas Regiments that had fought so gallantly as infantry at Corinth also had their horses returned, an occasion which set off uninhibited celebrations in the camps.

The Texas Brigade was organized with the Third, Sixth and Ninth Regiments and Whitfield's Texas Legion. The Arkansas Regiment's horses were in bad shape, therefore, they were not brigaded but were used as a separate regiment in forward scouting between Lumpkin's Mill and Holly Springs. They obtained some combat training during this period in that they fought several running skirmishes with Federal Cavalry probing the Confederate outpost north of Lumpkin's Mill.

At this time a change of command occurred in the district. Van Dorn was relieved and was appearing before a court of inquiry resulting from the bloodbath at Corinth. General John C. Pemberton was appointed in his place. In the meantime, General Ulysses S. Grant, the hero of Fort Donelson and Shiloh, at the head of an army of seventy-five thousand men was moving southward down the Mississippi Central Railroad. New Orleans had fallen to the Federal Navy and this victorious force was now standing below the Rebel forts at Vicksburg and Port Hudson. At the north end of the line, Memphis was the base of Federal operations on the Mississippi. Grant's aim was to capture and reduce the forts at Vicksburg and Port Hudson, thus opening up the Mississippi from source to mouth thus cutting the Confederacy in half. His initial effort was a direct overland route from LaGrange, Tennessee down the Mississippi Central Railroad, through Holly Springs, Oxford, Grenada and on to Vicksburg from the landside. His massive force crawled forward down the railroad with Pemberton's ineffective Rebels retreating slowly in his front until the Yalobusha was crossed and a stand made at Grenada. Though re-enforcements were daily arriving to bolster Pemberton's Army, it was a mere trickle compared to what was necessary if he was to long maintain the security of the state. Meanwhile, General Braxton Bragg had lost his nerve at the height of an eminently successful campaign in Kentucky; and, after the Battle of Perryville in that state, had retreated into central Tennessee and now was holed up at Murphreesboro. Another mighty Federal Army under General W. S. Rosecrans was building at Nashville and making preparations to move against Bragg. Under these circumstances the Confederate War Department was scraping the barrel to find men to thwart these two offensives in addition to supporting Lee in Virginia.

In mid-December Lieutenant Colonel John S. Griffith commanding the Texas Cavalry Brigade came up with the magic solution to one of the major problems. The Confederates were aware that Grant had established his main base of supply at Holly Springs. At this point his quartermaster had collected the mountain of supplies necessary to keep an army the size of Grant's in the field. Griffith figured that if all the scattered cavalry could be brought together under one command and a lightning raid conducted against Holly Springs, it would measurably reduce the effectiveness of Grant's winter offensive.

Griffith, accompanied by his regimental commanders, presented this plan to Pemberton who promptly approved it. When asked who he thought should command such an expedition, Griffith immediately replied, "General Van Dorn." Griffith argued that Van Dorn had an established reputation as a cavalryman in the old army and, further, Van Dorn had been acquitted by the board of inquiry and was currently without a command. The plan was approved. Van Dorn was called in and a raid on Holly Springs went into the planning stage.

This was indeed a propitious time for the effort against

Confederate Cavalrymen of the Western Army

Typical Federal Cavalryman

Grant's communications on the Mississippi Central. General Nathan Bedford Forrest and his hard riding legions were at this very time behind Union lines in west Tennessee playing havoc with the railroads and garrisons that were hauling Grant's supplies across that state.

Van Dorn called in the scattered cavalry to assist his best unit, the Texas Brigade. Colonel W. H. Jackson's Brigade arrived in the camp composed of the Fourth and Twenty-eighth Mississippi, Seventh Tennessee and Ballantines' Mississippi Regiment. When Lieutenant Colonel Robert McCullough rode in he had two small regiments, the First Mississippi and the Second Missouri. The Third Arkansas was sorted out as a result of the poor condition of the mounts and not every man was called. Some companies such as "A" and "K" were selected in full while some companies furnished only eight or ten men and one or two officers. When their organization was complete they made up a respectable battalion and were assigned to McCullough's Brigade.

On the night of December 16th, Van Dorn called in his brigade commanders. He told them the purpose of the organization and swore them to absolute secrecy. Under no circumstances was any man to be told their destination or intention. Late that evening the camps were thrown into an uproar by a sudden volley of shots from the First Mississippi area. There was a wild scramble for the guns and pandemonium ensued. McCullough blistered the atmosphere when he discovered the cause. The Mississippians' campfire had spread to a stump on which several men had hung their ammunition pouches and rifles. The resulting fire had exploded the cartridges scattering men in all directions.

On the afternoon of the 16th of December orders were issued to prepare for the field. Three days' rations were to be cooked and packed in saddlebags, and eighty rounds of ammunition were to be issued to each man. Throughout the day of the 17th, there was much speculation as to the destination and mission of the raiders. When sunset came, the men still did not know where they were going but "boots and saddles" was ringing through the camps. By darkness thirty-five hundred mounted Rebels were heading eastward in a column of fours. It was fast marching order and no artillery was taken along. The chief guess among the troopers was that they were to catch and destroy Colonel Theo Dickey's Federal Cavalrymen who had been smashing the Mobile and Ohio Railroad in the Tupelo area.

By daylight the fast riding horsemen were across the Yalo-

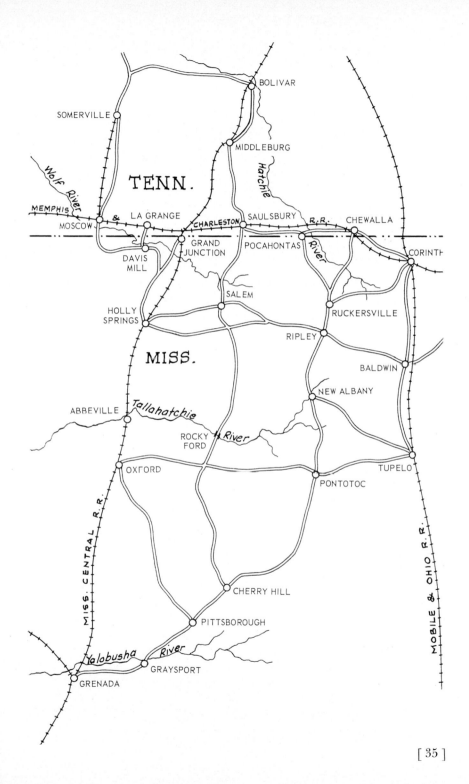

busha at Graysport and the little villages of Pittsborough and Cherry Hill were far to the rear. At mid-morning a halt was called to rest and feed the horses. Van Dorn soon had them back in the saddle and at noon the dusty column rode into Pontotoc. The word spread like wildfire that their own men were approaching the town so the good ladies turned out en masse, each with gifts of food in great variety. No halt was allowed and the long column pressed on through at a rapid clip. The women ran along side with their baskets from which the troopers grabbed anything their hands could hold and rode on northward.

A few miles north of town scouts galloped in to report that Dickey's bluecoats were approaching the column on the Tupelo Road. Every man expected to stand and fight since Dickey was their own chosen enemy. Instead of fighting, however, the pace was quickened and the raiders moved on. Dickey was of the same opinion as the Confederate privates; he, therefore, bore to the right to strike the New Albany Road north of Pontotoc. Reaching the road his advance guard collided with Van Dorn's rear-guard capturing three of the gray clad troopers. When a hard riding courier, going full tilt past a miles long column of horsemen, reported to Van Dorn in the lead that a battle was in progress in the rear, Van Dorn said, "Are they still in the rear?"

"Yes, Sir," the courier said.

"Well, you go back and tell your Colonel that the Yanks are where I want them, in the rear."

The column pushed on through the day always in sight of Federal scouts hanging on their flanks. After nightfall on the 18th a halt was called to obtain a much needed rest for exhausted men who had been falling asleep in the saddle. A terrible storm developed during the night, but despite torrential rains the weary men slept on.

At daylight on the 19th the column was once again in the saddle and pushing northward. Scouts were sent out in every direction to watch for pursuers and to guard the roads front and rear. At this time, too, Van Dorn sent for men among the raiders who were acquainted with the town of Holly Springs and the immediate vicinity. A rest halt was called in the late afternoon giving plenty of time for men and animals to consume a filling meal. By the time the command was back on the road, Van Dorn had been informed by a scout that all was serene in Holly Springs and the garrison was not aware of any impending danger.

Heading out north of Ripley to assure any alert Yankee scouts that he was still northbound, Van Dorn doubled back after dark. Using little known roads and by-paths, the hurrying column entered the westbound road to Holly Springs. A rapid pace was now set, the Rebel Raiders pounding along the roads until near midnight. Just short of Holly Springs Van Dorn split the command routing the Texas Brigade on a rough by-road in the direction of the town then pressed on with the main column. The General had issued orders that both columns were to halt just short of Holly Springs and await the hour of dawn to strike. It was a bitter cold night and men and horses shivered in the frigid air.

At the appointed hour the ghostly riders were once again moving forward. McCullough's Brigade had the point and pressed steadily on. The orders were that McCullough's Mississippians were to charge mounted through the Federal infantry and assail the cavalry, while the Second Missouri, assisted by the Third Arkansas Battalion, were to come in on foot and attack any infantryman in a mood to fight. Griffith's Texans were to come in from the east, sieze the railroad station and block any roads to prevent the escape of the garrison. Jackson's Brigade was to strike the north side of town, seal it off and defend the daiders. As the first streak of dawn broke over the Mississippi countryside, the Rebel Raiders thundered into town.

Colonel Robert C. Murphy, the Federal Commander of Holly Springs, had been warned by Grant that the raiding column might well be striking for his base. He was also warned to hold Colonel Quincy McNeil's Second Illinois Cavalry in readiness to assist in locating Van Dorn's troopers. The execution of this order was delayed till after daylight. Murphy did have some warning. A local negro had reported to him that a heavy force of Rebel horsemen was approaching. Murphy immediately dispatched runners to alert his garrison to stand to arms and prepare to defend themselves. They didn't make it. Griffith's Texans were on them at full charge before they could get their clothes on. In a matter of seconds Colonel Murphy and part of his garrison were in the bag. On the other side of town the First Mississippi riding full tilt tore through the tent area of the One hundred and first Illinois, firing into the faces of these bewildered Federals scrambling about in their underwear. They then pressed on to the fairgrounds to attack the Federal Cavalry. Before the now panicked infantry could collect their wits, the Missourians and Arkansans were upon them. Even so, a heavy volley of shots was fired before the Federals threw down their arms and surrendered. At the fairgrounds McNeil had gotten his men into the saddles. Without hesitation he counter-charged the oncoming Mississippians. A bloody melee swirled about the fairgrounds. Slashing sabers and popping pistols emptied saddles on both sides before part of the Federals could cut their way through and flee the town at racing speed. The largest military depot in the western military theater was now in the hands of Van Dorn's Rebels.

When the smoke of the fighting had died away, Privates J. E. Christian and John H. Casteel were down, wounded. Casteel was too badly wounded to be moved, was left behind, and fell into the hands of the enemy.

The systematic destruction of the depot was now commenced. It was a haul indeed. Thousands of tons of rifles, pistols, blankets, medicines, clothing and other military property were stacked in every available building that could be used as a warehouse. This was put to the torch. In one instance tons of ammunition were piled in the square, part of it in front of the Federal Hospital. Despite the pleas of the Federal Medical Officer in Charge, it was fired. The resulting explosions blew out windows and doors seriously injuring some of the patients. Plundering became a high-handed game. With the exception of security details posted on the various roads leading to Holly Springs, every man was newly outfitted from underwear to boots. New Colts Army Six-shooters were stuck three at a time in the belts of some of the raiders. From 6 a. m. until near sunset the destruction went on apace. The fire from the burning stores spread to some of the town's dwellings, leveling most of the buildings on the public square.

Among some uninvited guests discovered in the town was Mrs. Julia Dent Grant, wife of the enemy commander. She was protected in her person and her dwelling by guards posted from the Texas Brigade.

Just after sunset the victorious Rebels were in the saddle and moving northward. For many, many miles up the northbound road, the fiery reflection of the Holly Springs destruction glowed in the evening sky. Van Dorn had paroled 1500 Federal prisoners and had destroyed nearly a million dollars worth of irreplaceable military equipment. This was the most destructive single cavalry raid of the Civil War and was to accomplish exactly what Griffith had predicted—Grant's withdrawal from northern Mississippi and the abandonment of his campaign.

Van Dorn's intention now was to move into Tennessee destroying the railroads at LaGrange, Middleburg and Bolivar, thus completing the work begun by Forrest. At the Coldwater River a few miles north of Holly Springs Van Dorn intended to burn the railroad bridge. The Federal guards refused to surrender when demanded to do so; therefore, the raiders by-passed the bridge and went into camp a few miles beyond. The next day was cold and clear and the troops were early on the road. The next stop was Davis Mill on the Wolf River a few miles south of LaGrange. Here was an important position embracing a railroad bridge, road bridge and grist mill. It was heavily guarded by Colonel William H. Morgan and his Twenty-fifth Indiana Infantry. These were no milkfed soldiers as Van Dorn was soon to learn. They refused to surrender and stood their ground. The Texas Brigade was dismounted and sent forward to pen down the defenders in the Blockhouse and trenches. The rest of the command was deployed on three sides of the place to close in once the Texans had done their job. The entire effort proved futile. The river was impassable since the Federals commanded the bridge and all approaches leading to it. A weary afternoon was spent searching for a weak spot in the Federal defense to no avail. The Third Arkansas with their Missouri Comrades-in-arms were pinned down for some time losing several men in the process. Among these was Private Miles Van Sickel who was grieviously wounded and left behind for the Federals to pick up. At sunset the venture was called off. The command withdrew under fire losing several more men killed and wounded before they could get to their horses.

Camp was made after dark at the Tennessee line. By now the flag was up. The Federal telegraph lines between every Federal post in west Tennessee were humming. Colonel Mizner of Grant's Cavalry had not moved with sufficient speed to satisfy the General. He was, therefore, relieved and Colonel Benjamin Grierson had been given his command. Colonel A. L. Lee with his brigade was pounding northward. An infantry corps was split up and dispatched in several directions in hopes of intercepting the hard riding Rebels. Van Dorn's timing was perfect. Forrest's raid into west Tennessee had badly scattered the opposition and they had not yet had time to react to Van Dorn's raid.

At daybreak on the 22nd the Rebels struck the Memphis and Charleston Railroad at Moscow. Miles of railroad track were laid waste and the Rebels moved on toward Somerville. At this place a Tennessee Unionist meeting was broken up and the Confederate sympathizers plied the still moving horsemen with every type of fine food. In the meantime, the confused Federals were gathering their strength far to the rear at Holly Springs. Since the ghostly riders could not be found or fought, the Federals were now laying plans to intercept the raiders on their return to Mississippi. By early morning of Christmas Day the hard riding Grierson now re-enforced by the Third Michigan, was closing in. Both columns were headed for Bolivar, Tennessee.

Approaching Bolivar from the north, Van Dorn encountered the Federal force. He moved to the attack. The Texas Brigade was sent forward to drive in the Federal pickets. This they did in full charge. Gaining the town, the Texans dismounted and moved against the now thoroughly barricaded and defended town. Van Dorn realized that he was getting himself bogged down in a fire fight at a time when he needed to be moving southward and recalled the Texans. Remounting this brigade, he sent them southward to attack Middleburg seven miles away while the balance of his command kept the Federals pinned in Bolivar. The subsequent assault on the fortified town of Middleburg cost the Texans some twenty men in killed and wounded. Van Dorn, coming up with the main body, called off the assault after satisfying himself that the Yankees were firmly fixed in position.

With the opposition again in the rear, the Rebels now moved southward. His intention was to threaten the Federals in the direction of Corinth in order to fix that garrison in place, thus opening a hole for escape across the Memphis and Charleston Railroads. Colonel Grierson was now alerted to Van Dorn's tactics and, calling in his garrisons from Bolivar to Middleburg, started in pursuit. Grierson notified Grant that the Rebel column was composed of 7000 troops and were moving in the direction of Saulsbury. His over-estimation of Van Dorn's force was indication enough of his reluctance to close with the Rebels and give battle .By the time Grierson rode into Saulsbury the rear of the Rebel column and disappeared into Mississippi.

Grant now began firing off telegrams in every direction. He ordered his infantry to occupy Salem; the Second Illinois Cavalry to move eastward to Holly Springs; and Hatch's Cavalry to move eastward from Oxford to prevent the Rebels escape across Rocky Ford on the Tallahatchie.

By the time Mudd's Blue Horsemen reached Salem the

hard riding Rebels had long since passed and moved on to Ripley. Mudd doubled back and rode at a gallop toward Ripley where he was joined by Mizner's Regiment, both moving on into town. They were too late. Van Dorn, after halting the exhausted raiders to eat a belated Christmas Dinner, had moved southward out of the town and camped as the Federal advance moved in from the north. The Federal Commander was sure he had the raiders in the bag. Just before daylight he received the bad news. The Confederate "campfires" had been nothing more than large blazes kept going by Rebel rearguard troops. The main Confederate column was already approaching Rocky Ford far away to the south.

This night march insured Van Dorn's escape. Slipping past Hatch at Rocky Ford, the slippery Rebels turned eastward again to Pontotoc. The night of the 26th was indeed a miserable night for weary men. In a pouring driving rain the benumbed Confederates nodded in the saddle while the footsore horses stumbled on. At Pontotoc as at Ripley the Federals arrived too late. Twelve days after leaving the camps at Grenada the eminently successful Confederate Raiders were back in camp.

The Holly Springs raid was the most destructive single cavalry raid of the Civil War. In addition to this heavy loss, Van Dorn's destruction of the railroads caused Grant's withdrawal from Mississippi and postponed the fall of Vicksburg by six months. The Holly Springs raid had also produced a second advantage. The green horsemen were now veteran cavalrymen honed to sharpness on the fighting fields.

Chapter V

Shortly after the new year began, Van Dorn reorganized the Cavalry Division in preparation for movement to central Tennessee. Grant was no longer a threat and Bragg was sorely in need of the mounted arm on his flanks at Murfreesboro; thus, all the available cavalry in Mississippi was to move forward to the active theater. The final grouping of the cavalry gave the Third Arkansas a crack commander, Brigadier General Frank C. Armstrong. His brigade consisted of the Third Arkansas under Colonel S. G. Earle; Second Kentucky commanded by Colonel T. G. Woodward; First Tennessee with Colonel J. T. Wheeler; and the First Tennessee Battalion under Major Charles McDonald. The Texas Brigade was assigned to Brigadier General J. W. Whitfield and consisted of the old command of the Third, Sixth, Ninth Texas and the Texas Legion. These two brigades were assigned to Brigadier General W. H. Jackson as a division. Van Dorn was to be joined in Tennessee by the brigades of Brigadier Generals N. B. Forrest and Will T. Martin and Colonel G. W. Cosby. This organization was designated a Cavalry Corps and was to occupy the left wing of the Confederate Army of Tennessee.

The camps at Grenada were left behind in early February and a slow, leisurely march was made to Tennessee. On February 16, 1863, the Arkansans rode into the sleepy village of Spring Hill to enter upon new fields of duty. The early Spring was given over to scouting and patroling along the roads from Spring Hill northward toward Franklin leading to several sharp skirmishes with the probing blue horsemen. In late February headquarters

Maj. Gen. W. H. Jackson

Brig. General Frank C. Armstrong

Brig. General J. W. Whitfield

were shifted to Columbia where the command was given a long rest to recoup the horses and refit for the Spring campaign that was sure to open as soon as the roads dried sufficiently to allow for military movement over the countryside.

While Van Dorn rested his main force in the area of Columbia, the never idle Forrest ranged far into central Tennessee probing the Federal lines as far forward as Nashville. His repeated admonition to Van Dorn that the Federals would be coming out was justified in early March.

Rosecrans, becoming increasingly apprehensive as to the plans and purposes of the Confederate Army, ordered a reconnaissance in force to proceed down the railroad toward Columbia and others toward Chapel Hill and Spring Hill. His purpose was immediately devined by Forrest and reported to Van Dorn. The main effort by the Federals was in the direction of Columbia thus it was this column that Van Dorn elected to strike. There were in the Federal column 2,837 men which included 600 cavalry, the Eighteenth Ohio Battery of six guns and near 2,000 infantry. The senior colonel, John Coburn, of the Thirty-third Indiana was in command.

Coburn was a brave man. With only a vague notion what was in his front, he pressed relentlessly on. Forrest's troopers, lurking on the flanks of the Federals, were highly impressed by the eight-miles long column of cavalry, artillery and infantry followed by 80 foraging wagons. Forrest had no intention of bringing on a general engagement with so formidable a force and confined himself to periodic shelling and nuisance attacks on the column. Meanwhile, Van Dorn called in his scattered brigades and concentrated astride the Federal line of march at Thompson's Station. By late evening of the 4th, he had at hand the brigades of Frank C. Armstrong, G. W. Cosby, Will T. Martin and J. W. Whitfield. At darkness he was joined by Forrest bringing his fighting strength to near 6,000 men. Van Dorn's Artillery was all at hand in the organizations of Captain S. L. Freeman's six guns and Captain Houston King's Missouri Battery also of six guns. The two antagonists bivouacked within sight of each other and settled down for the night.

At daylight on March 5th Van Dorn had his troops in line Despite the fact that he outnumbered his opponents nearly two to one, he waited on the defensive. Coburn, realizing that he was a long way from his base and without support, made a decision more brave than wise. He elected to attack. Sending most of his supply train back to Franklin in order to divest himself of any encumbrance, he advanced toward Thompson's Station. The Thirty-third and Eighty-fifth Indiana formed his right and the Twenty-second Wisconsin and Nineteenth Michigan held the left. The minor portion of the cavalry was posted dismounted under Colonel Thomas Jordan in rear of the infantry files. In this position, Coburn assailed Van Dorn at 10 a. m. Van Dorn had ordered King's Battery run forward by hand to the front of his line adjacent to a stonewall. He then sent Whitfield's Brigade to the wall to support the battery. As the action opened, the Third Arkansas was dismounted and advanced to the support of Whitfield.

Coburn's right, advancing in gallant style, aimed square for the pounding battery of King. The Federal Batteries opened all along the front with a rapid discharge of shell and case shot, the infantry blasting away with rifle fire as they came on. At this point Forrest, swinging wide around the Federal left, ordered Starnes' and Edmonson's Regiments to charge the dismounted Yankee Cavalrymen and drive them off their hill. This was done in full charge. Freeman's Battery was then sent up the hill where they unlimbered in full view of the entire Federal force and opened a fearful fire into their flank and rear. With the advent of Nathan Bedford Forrest on their left flank, the entire blue cavalry fled the field followed by an infantry regiment that broke and scattered.

The charging Federal front line was within two hundred yards of the stonewall when Whitfield and Earle rose up and poured a destructive volley into them cutting down nearly the entire front file. Van Dorn, galloping along the wall screamed out, "CHARGE—CHARGE!" The timing was perfect. Before the shocked Federals could recover from the first Rebel volley, Whitfield's Brigade and the Third Arkansas were over the wall. Coburn's command precipitately left the field. Back down the hill, through the village and up the opposing slope they went with Whitfield and Earle popping away at them with every opportunity to halt and reload. On the crest of the ridge Coburn halted. The Nineteenth Michigan and the Twenty-second Wisconsin packed in behind the Indiana men and here they stood. Armstrong's entire Brigade was now in the fray and followed Whitfield and the Third Arkansas into the Federal lines. Six-shooters, bayonets and rifle butts were all employed with murderous fury until the battered Rebels drew off down the slope. Armstrong's Brigade Battle Flag was left in the hands of the Wisconsin men. As soon as the disordered files could be reorganized, Armstrong led them back in again. This time they had some assistance. Forrest's Brigade, having gained the Federal rear, charged into them at full speed. The rear files broke and scattered to the woods, many of them being shot in the process. Somewhere in the last melee, Colonel Earle was shot through the head at point blank range killing him instantly. With the screaming, yelling troopers of Forrest riding down his rear and the Arkansans and Texans battering at his front, Coburn threw down his sword and called for quarter.

General Forrest ordered an immediate pursuit of the fleeing remnants of the Federal Command but reaped few results. Only twenty-five men were captured, the balance making far too rapid a retreat to be overtaken. Losses on both sides were heavy considering the short space of time involved in the actual fighting. In addition to the death of Colonel Earle of the Third Arkansas, Colonel Trezevant of Forrest's Command was killed in the last minutes of the contest. Altogether the Third Arkansas lost 6 killed and 28 wounded including three excellent junior officers, Captain Stephen Jester and Lieutenant E. D. Ward were killed, and Captains J. F. Earle and W. H. Blackwell and Lieutenants Hines and Cleaver were wounded.

The total Confederate loss was 357 whereas the Federals gave up 1,500 in killed, wounded and captured including Colonels Coburn and Jordan. The fire-eating Forrest had his horse shot from under him in the last charge and making a flying dismount, continued the charge on foot. To the unfeigned joy of the Third Arkansas, Armstrong's Brigade was assigned to this soldier's soldier at the close of the Battle of Thompson's Station.

Though Thompson's Station was a resounding Confederate success, the fruits of the fight were less than overwhelming. Had Forrest been in Van Dorn's shoes it is highly unlikely that any of the Federals would have escaped the holocaust. It is probable that Forrest would have taken a much bigger force than that alloted to him in this fight, gained the Federal rear and bagged them all in one fell swoop. His tactics past and future sustain this point. The day following the fight, Lieutenant Colonel Anson W. Hobson was promoted Colonel of the Third Arkansas; Major M. J. Henderson went to Lieutenant Colonel and Captain W. F. Earle moved to Major. Lieutenant W. S. Parks moved up to Captain of "F" Company and A. B. Duke was promoted to Captain of "E" Company. At the close of this reorganization and the reassignment to Forrest's Division, the Third Arkansas

Lieut. General Nathan Bedford Forrest

said farewell to General Earl Van Dorn. This proved to be a final farewell in that General Van Dorn was assassinated a short time later by an irate husband of an alleged "wronged" woman. The assassin walked into Van Dorn's Headquarters tent and shot him where he sat. Right or wrong, the killer was never brought to trial.

There was little respite for Forrest's Division following the action at Thompson's Station. Van Dorn, taking his own division with him, withdrew from the battle area toward Columbia with the captured prisoners and materiel. Forrest was ordered forward to the area of Rutherford Creek to check the advance of another heavy Federal column advancing in that direction. Forrest had left Starnes' Brigade and the Third Arkansas at Thompson's Station as pickets to cover Van Dorn's withdrawal. They were assailed by a heavy force of infantry and cavalry under the redoubtable General Phillip H. Sheridan. A slow, skillful retrograde movement was made by Starnes, fighting at every wall and hill until he reached the safety of the main command at Spring Hill at nightfall.

On the 11th Sheridan reached the fords on Rutherford Creek with Minty's and Smith's Brigades where he found pickets of the Second Kentucky on guard. Minty's efforts to cross the fast running stream resulted in the killing of several of his troopers and failure. Late in the day, Sheridan with all his force reached the creek at the same time that Forrest reached the opposite bank. The Federals opened with artillery, shelling the woods vigorously, driving the Rebels to cover and allowing the infantry to cross unmolested. Sheridan now formed his brigades and advanced on Starnes and Armstrong. Forrest surveying the field with his practiced eye, could see that no advantage could be gained from taking on this large force in pitched battle. Once again he resorted to delaying and confusing the enemy. His rapid maneuvering and sporadic attacks caused Sheridan to call off the action at sunset allowing the Rebels to escape southward. On reaching the Duck River, Forrest found the pontoon bridge destroyed by high water which securely stranded him on the north bank. Not to be check-mated, he rode westward in a long, tiring night march and crossed the river twenty-five miles downstream joining the main force late the following day.

The same day that Forrest joined Van Dorn, Sheridan returned to the area of Franklin. Forrest lost no time in camp. By March 15th he was back at Spring Hill and probing the

Yankee outposts along the Harpeth. From this position, the intrepid scouts of Starnes' Brigade brought in information that two Federal units were in and near the village of Brentwood, nine miles above Franklin, and were a sufficient distance apart to warrant an effort to take them. This program was immediately put into action. On March 24th, Starnes was ordered to cross the Harpeth above Franklin; strike and destroy the railroad leading to Brentwood; wreck the telegraph lines; assail the Nineteenth Michigan in their stockade; and block their retreat in the direction of Nashville. Forrest was to come up with Armstrong's Brigade and the artillery at daylight, forming on the right of Starnes. His intention was to capture the Twenty-second Wisconsin in the redoubt in the forks of the Wilson and Franklin Pikes.

At midnight Starnes was across the Harpeth and striking for the railroad. His orders to capture the Federal pickets without gunfire was not successful. The Federals became alarmed, fired into the raiding party and fled into Franklin. General Gordon Grainger, now apprised of his danger, dispatched General Green Clay Smith's Brigade in the direction of Brentwood and began hammering out the warning over the telegraph.

By daylight Starnes had torn up the railroad and destroyed the telegraph lines and was within rifle-shot of the Michigan stronghold. Here he awaited the arrival of Forrest. The Chief was late. A great deal of difficulty had been encountered getting the guns across the Harpeth and Forrest was an hour overdue. Starnes, fearing entrapment in his position, drew off to the Hillsborough Pike and learned to his mortification that Forrest and Armstrong had just passed on another road pounding in the direction of Brentwood.

On reaching the rendezvous point Forrest discovered the absence of Starnes but, completely uninhibited, moved to assail the garrison in Brentwood. Two companies of the Tenth Tennessee were left to guard his rear and another two companies were routed around the town to prevent escape of the enemy. Armstrong was ordered to deploy to the left of the road and attack the town while Forrest, with his escort and the balance of the Tennessee men, moved off to the right. At this point, a Federal courier rode full tilt into the escort and was captured. He was bearing a request for help from Colonel Bloodgood to Grainger in Franklin. The Federal pickets were driven in with a rush and Forrest was before the town. At this point Forrest attempted his now famous ruse. Sending in Major Charles Anderson under flag of truce, he demanded the immediate and unconditional surrender of the garrison or he, "would give no quarter if required to take the place by storm." This invitation, Bloodgood refused. Signaling to Armstrong to assault the rear of the fort, Forrest dismounted his escort and six companies of the Tenth Tennessee and moved in.

The Third Arkansas, Second Kentucy and First Tennessee formed line dismounted and moved out. At this point Bloodgood had hitched up his teams and intended to make a run for it in hopes of escaping to Nashville. His drivers crashed into the Third Arkansas blocking the road. The Arkansans made short shrift of the wagon train and in a matter of minutes were securely lodged in the Yankee outworks. Freeman's battery was wheeled into battery position between the Arkansans and Kentuckians all within one hundred yards of the enemy garrison. The firing from the side being attacked by Forrest was brief and sporadic— then silence. Bloodgood in his report said that he had been pressed back into his works and that two cannon were aimed point-blank at his people, thus he felt obliged to surrender the garrison to prevent unnecessary effusion of blood. The Rebels raked in 520 men of the Twenty-second Wisconsin and large quantities of supplies of all kinds. The Arkansans left Brentwood largely equipped with new revolvers, boots, blankets and many with spirited horses to replace the worn out animals they had been riding. There was not a single man in the Confederate force wounded or lost in the action.

Armstrong's Brigade was detailed to take the prisoners and property to safety on the Hillsborough Pike, move as rapidly as possible to the rear and to destroy what could not be removed from Brentwood. The Third Arkansas headed the column, guarding the prisoners while the Tennessee and Kentucky men brought up the rear with the captured wagons. In the meanwhile, Forrest, with the balance of the command, rode pell-mell to the Harpeth River Stockade and the Nineteenth Michigan. Wheeling up the guns he ordered a shot fired into the fort. The cloud of flying splinters and dust was still unsettled when Major Anderson appeared in front of the garrison with his not-too-clean shirt attached to his sabre. His message from Forrest was cryptic and understandable. "I have you completely surrounded and will blow Hell out of you in five minutes and won't take one of you alive if I have to sacrifice my men in storming this stockade." Captain Basset promptly surrendered himself and 275 men. The prisoners were hurried off to the Hillsborough Pike and the railroad bridge was burned.

The long column of friend and foe was less than five miles from Brentwood when General Green Clay Smith came on the scene. With the Second Michigan, Ninth Pennsylvania and the Fourth and Sixth Kentucky (Union), Smith pulled into the town to survey the smouldering wreckage. Discovering the route of Forrest's retreat, he rode rapidly in pursuit.

The Tenth Tennessee riding at the rear of the Confederate column was the first to see the enemy. Smith, riding at the head of the Sixth Kentucky, came up on several of Armstrong's stragglers in the road and routed them in a panic. These worthies, without firing a single shot in warning, rode full tilt into the Tenth Tennessee crowding men off the road and tangling up the rear of the column. The Tennessee men had no chance of recovery. The Federals in a column of fours, sabres drawn, thundered up the road at full speed and rode over them. Colonel Gordon of the Fourth Mississippi, swung his men off the road and attempted to form line, facing rear, but was driven back mingling with the Tenth Tennessee. Colonel Hobson at the head of the column heard the rapid discharge of carbines and pistols from the rear and ordered the Third Arkansas to move "on right, by fours into line—WHEEL!" and hold. In this position he checked the rout of the Mississippi and Tennessee men. Forrest, in a towering rage, seized a double-barreled shotgun from a passing trooper and fired both barrels into a mass of fleeing fugitives. This act stopped the miscreants in their tracks.

In the midst of the panic Starnes, who had been absent since daylight, rode on the scene. Without hesitation and still at a gallop, he formed right-by-fours into line and charged. The panic shoe was now on the other foot. Doubling the Federal column back on itself like a wet rope, he smashed Smith's entire brigade. The horse race continued back into the outskirts of Brentwood before Forrest called off the pursuit. Smith's only accomplishment was killing two men and capturing nineteen and burning three of the captured wagons. Not one Federal prisoner was lost. When Forrest toted up the score at Columbia he had 758 prisoners and large quantities of much needed supplies at a cost of four killed, sixteen wounded and nineteen captured. The Brentwood affair was a signal success.

Chapter VI

March 25th to April 9th was a period of comparative quiet on the Confederate left. The weary horsemen had time to regroup, refit and care for the ailing horses. Both major armies still lay idle, glaring at each other over their cavalry patrols. Bragg in front of Wartrace and Rosecrans at Murfreesboro were both ill-disposed to create any big problems that may bring on a fight. The daily reports with the cryptic ending, "all quiet along the lines," applied only to the major infantry units. In the cavalry front, the pickets listened daily to the shrill whistle of Minie balls and the occasional screech of a shell as snipers took a crack at each other. A lot of good men lost their lives in this "quiet" war, the only major loss being to their families at home.

On April 10th, Van Dorn broke the quiet. Bragg was getting nervous about the keen Federal activity on his far right where General Joseph Wheeler's Cavalry held the line. Bragg then ordered Van Dorn to move forward to Franklin, probe the Federal lines, devine their intention and to create a diversion for his hard pressed horsemen on his right. To this purpose Van Dorn with Generals W. H. Jackson and Forrest's Divisions moved on Franklin. The Commanding General rode with Jackson's Division on the main pike from Columbia to Franklin while Forrest kept close to the Harpeth River on the Lewisburg Pike. This move was obviously a diversion since no attempt at secrecy was made and the Federals had plenty of warning of their coming. General Gordon Grainger had called to Rosecrans for help the day before the appearance of the Rebels, which summons was answered by the dispatch of General D. S. Stanley's crack Cavalry

Brigade from Triune to Franklin. The arrival of this unit proved to be Van Dorn's undoing.

At 10 a. m. Jackson assailed the Ohio Infantry guarding the approaches to the town and drove them back into the buildings and fort. At the same time, Armstrong's Brigade dismounted and drove in the pickets on the Lewisburg Pike. Here two events occurred which demonstrated the sometimes comic aspects of what is otherwise a dirty and dangerous business. Grainger admitted that the attack was pressed with such lack of vigor that he concluded it was a diversion and that Brentwood was once again the main target. At this time he received a panicked dispatch from the Brentwood Garrison that their pickets had been driven in. Grainger, in his formal report, says that he dispatched General Green Clay Smith's Cavalry Brigade at top speed to Brentwood to rescue the garrison. On arrival at the scene, Smith discovered that the pickets had been driven in by four negroes walking along the road. The folks at Brentwood must have been a little nervous.

With his main mounted force now beyond his reach, Grainger's hope rested with Stanley who was approaching the field. At this juncture Stanley's extension of orders, bordering on disobedience, nearly cost Forrest half his command. Stanley, who was supposed to report directly to Grainger in the town north of the Harpeth River, elected to by-pass the town; strike for the river at Hughes' Mill; cross and assail the rear of the Confederate force. Forrest was in front of Franklin with Armstrong's Brigade and two of Freeman's guns while the balance of his division followed up on the Lewisburg Pike In the approaching column, Biffle's Regiment rode in front, followed by Captain Freeman and his remaining four guns, with the balance of Starnes' Brigade strung out along the pike. In the area of Hughes' Mill the Pike parallels the river for some distance and it was on this stretch that Stanley debouched.

Freeman's artillerists were loafing along, legs thrown carelessly over the saddle pommel, evidencing no hurry since they knew they were not sorely needed up front. Witnesses said that Captain Freeman suddenly sat bolt upright in the saddle, yelled to the cannoneers to drop trails and go "action front" to the right. A mad scramble was made for limber linkage and rammers just as Stanley's men burst from the trees and, crossing a narrow field, rode full charge into the guns. One Confederate gunner said that he had rammed home a charge, inserted the primer and yanked the lanyard, but the primer was faulty and the gun failed to fire. The next second he was knocked flat on his back by a charging horse. Freeman's four guns and thirty-six prisoners were in the hands of the Federals in less time than it takes to tell it. Starnes up front with Biffle, hearing the sudden burst of firing, doubled back at a dead run and came on the scene just as the Fourth US Regulars were driving the prisoners back toward the river. The rear of the Rebel column also came up at this time and, joining in the chase, put the Federals back over the ford at a run. All of the guns and most of the prisoners were recaptured in the chase, but Forrest suffered one hard loss in the fracas.

Captain S. L. Freeman, a gallant man of proven ability, while being driven to the rear at pistol-point, was told by the mounted Federal to run faster. Freeman replied that he could run no faster because of the heavy artillerist's boots he was wearing. The Federal promptly shot and killed him. A Doctor Skelton of Forrest's Staff was also shot at the same time but the bullet, passing through his hand when he threw it up begging not to be shot, was deflected. When Forrest came on the scene a few minutes later he jumped from his horse, took Freeman's hand in his to determine if he was really dead, then wept unashamedly. The Cavalry Corps of the Army of Tennessee never forgave or forgot the Fourth U. S. Regulars for this act and vented their wrath and vengeance on this unit at every opportunity for the rest of the war.

Van Dorn's total loss was 70 killed, wounded and missing including four wounded in the Arkansas Regiment. Grainger's loss was 23 killed, 33 wounded and 27 captured. No formal report was ever rendered by General Van Dorn on the action at Franklin. Shortly after this action he was killed by an assassin closing the book on a turbulent and controversial career. On the afternoon of the 11th, Forrest's Division was back in camp.

With the advent of Spring on the Tennessee line, the Federals bestirred themselves. General Rosecrans, after the disastrous draw fought with Bragg at Murfreesboro, had spent long months regrouping and refitting. He was now ready to move. First, he knew that if Bragg backed up into the fortress of Chattanooga, it would be a tough job dislodging him. Second, if Bragg's railroad to Atlanta and Knoxville was broken up, the Confederates might retreat all the way to Atlanta. As these considerations rattled around in Rosecran's mind, Colonel Abel D. Streight came forward with a program. Streight, Commander of the Fifty-first Indiana Cavalry, was a brave man but his scheme went a lot further than bravery. He proposed to hand-pick 2,000 officers and men; mount them on mules; ship the compliment by steamboat to the Mississippi-Alabama line; then strike out across Alabama for the railroads in Georgia below Chattanooga. From its inception the entire story reads like first-class fiction. Brigadier General James A. Garfield, (later to become President), gave the venture his blessing and persuaded his superiors to accept it. On April 10th, 1863, Streight moved out. On the 19th after a long and tortuous journey on the rivers of Tennessee, the "mule-borne" force disembarked at Eastport, Mississippi.

In the meantime, General Greenville M. Dodge with 7,500 men was to create a diversion in favor of Streight and assist him in getting a head start into the wilds of North Alabama. Dodge had his troubles when Confederate Brigadier General P. D. Roddy with one small brigade attacked him with such zeal and frequency that his move to join Streight was stalled twelve miles short of their rendezvous. In addition, Roddy's untamed group of mounted frontiersmen had a riotous time with Colonel Streight. They said that the braying of 2,000 mules was something to hear on a still night and consequently alerted every Confederate within twenty miles. They crept into his pens the first night Streight was on the ground and, screeching like Comanche Indians and firing pistols, stampeded the army of mules all over the county. Streight was delayed two days attempting to recover his stubborn chargers. This gave time for the story to reach the ears of Braxton Bragg and Nathan Bedford Forrest.

On April 23rd Forrest was ordered to take his old brigade and make for Decatur, Alabama; unite with Roddy; take command, and eliminate one Colonel Abel D. Streight. Leaving Armstrong's Brigade behind to guard the left of Bragg's Army, Forrest started south for Alabama and everlasting glory. On the 25th, Streight cut loose from the convoy of General Dodge at Tuscumbia and sallied forth. Here begins one of the great military stories of our time. The relentless Forrest tacked on to the rear of the Federal column on the 29th of April near Russellville, Alabama and for five days and nights fought them every hour giving them no rest; driving his own men remorselessly in the process. The pursuit went on for more than one hundred and fifty miles over swamps, mountains and forested plateaus until at Cedar Bluff, just short of the Georgia line, Streight and his totally exhausted force was driven to ground. Forrest had two small regiments and part of his faithful escort on their staggering horses at the finish, but compelled Streight to surrender his 1,700 man force to this Corporal's Guard of 450 weary men. Among many noted military experts who commented on this feat, General Lord Wolseley said that the pursuit and capture of Streight's Raiders was the greatest single exploit of mounted arms in the history of warfare. The "Wizard of the Saddle" had certainly earned his accolade.

On May 16th in pursuance of orders from General Bragg, Forrest was back at Spring Hill, Tennessee in command of the cavalry corps replacing the dead Earl Van Dorn. During his absence there had been a long period of relative quiet on the Middle Tennessee front, but now that he was back all was hustle and bustle again in the cavalry camps. At this time there occurred another bizarre incident in this strange war of bizarre incidents. During the pursuit of Streight, Forrest had had occasion to chastise a young Lieutenant for a minor infraction of discipline in the handling of an artillery piece. Forrest had transferred the officer to another command which, in the Lieutenant's mind, was a reflection on his courage. He therefore went to Columbia to seek redress. Forrest took him out into a hallway and heard the complaint, but still refused to relent. At this point, the Lieutenant drew his revolver, jammed it into Forrest's side and pulled the trigger. The bullet entered his left hip just above the joint, glanced off his pelvis, ploughed through his body and went into the wall. Forrest, quick as a cat, grasped the pistol with his right hand preventing a second shot; opened a pocket knife with his teeth that he had been carrying in his hand; rammed it into the boy's abdomen and ripped him open. The Lieutenant dropped his pistol and fled. Forrest walked across the street to his Surgeon and asked if his wound was mortal. When informed that he probably would not live, Forrest grabbed a pistol from a bystander and went in search of his assailant. He found him stretched on a counter in a store in a dying condition. The boy apologized and begged forgiveness. One witness said that Forrest promptly forgave him and, "Forrest wept like a child. It was the saddest of all the sad incidents of the long and bitter war I witnessed."

Forrest didn't die. In fact, he suffered very little from this terrible wound and was back in the saddle by the first of June spoiling for a fight. When he was informed that General Grainger had transferred his Command Headquarters from Franklin to Triune, Forrest determined to assail the garrison at Franklin in hopes of capturing them before Grainger could effect their rescue.

On June 4th the expedition was put in motion. Forrest took his old brigade under Colonel Starnes on the Columbia Pike and routed Armstrong's Brigade along the Lewisburg Pike with orders to cross the river above the town and hold the roads leading to Triune. With his accustomed dash, Forrest led a mounted charge right into the heart of the town where he had the men dismount. In a matter of minutes the artillerists were wheeling the guns along the street by hand, blasting away at the Federals in the fort. Forrest battered down the doors of the jail to release the civilian prisoners being held on political charges and cleaned the Federal storehouses of their contents. Here again occurred an "incident." Colonel J. P. Baird, Commander of the garrison, was frantically signaling to Grainger in Triune for help when Forrest mistook the signal flag for the usual surrender instrument. He promptly rode forward with his own flag of truce. A Federal soldier, crouching behind a fence, squinting down the sights of his rifle, recognized his famous target—Nathan Forrest. Instead of firing, he called out to Forrest by name to withdraw and shouted to him that the flag in sight was not a token of surrender. Forrest gallantly tipped his hat to his saviour and rode away.

While Forrest was sacking the town of Franklin, Armstrong was not so lucky. On crossing the Harpeth he had left Colonel Hobson and his Third Arkansas to guard the crossing, and proceeded on to the Triune Road with the balance of his brigade. While listening to the sound of Forrest's fight in Franklin, the rumble of hooves reached his ears coming from the direction of Triune. Federal Colonel A. P. Campbell was coming at a gallop to the relief of the garrison. Armstrong promptly deployed for battle. Campbell charged right in and the melee was on. Woodward's Battalion was driven slowly back on Armstrong's main force where the whole began a slow, fighting retreat toward the river. Campbell was not to be denied access to Franklin. The fighting was close and deadly as Armstrong's men valiantly resisted charge after charge as they backed slowly toward the crossing. At this point Colonel Hobson, realizing the position of his Chief, elected to cross the Harpeth and move to his assistance. Swinging wide of the road to the right, Hobson came up on a rise in ground and instantly the fighting field was in plain view. Armstrong's men were moving to his left and the Federals, now in a confused mass, were moving across his front in close pursuit. Hobson didn't hesitate. He commanded the regiment to "Right by fours—forward into line," and as soon as the last element trotted into position the commands of "Draw pistols—gallop——CHARGE!" rang on the air. Before the shocked Federals were fully aware of their presence, the Arkansans rode full charge into them. Pistols blazing, sabres swinging, hooves flailing, they rode through and over Campbell's Brigade, scattering them like frightened quail, then doubled back toward the river. There was no further opposition. Hobson held the river bank until the last man was over then rejoined his command. In this charge the Arkansans didn't get off so easy. Captain H. C. Cleaver of Company "H" was shot through the stomach and brought off across the saddle of Lieutenant Colonel Henderson. Cleaver died next day. Privates James K. P. Ballard, William S. Hoggins, Samuel James and William D. Williams were severely wounded, but were brought off by their comrades. Forrest, hearing the steady drumfire of close conflict drifting away southward, called off the attack on the Franklin garrison and retired down the Columbia Pike. Armstrong lost eighteen men captured and ten killed. The Federals lost ten killed in Hobson's charge including Colonel Faulkner of the Second Michigan. The Confederates went into bivouac near Spring Hill and camped unmolested.

Captain Cleaver's command of Company "H" had been short lived. He had succeeded to the post when Captain Alonzo Montgomery resigned on June 3rd. Three days after his promotion to Captain, Cleaver was dead. Lieutenant C. W. Leake was then promoted to Captain and assumed command of the company. There were several changes in the command structure of the Third Arkansas in the Spring of '63. Captain W. B. Keeton of Company "K" died and was replaced by Lieutenant M. H. Carden. In Company "I" Captain M. E. Davis resigned as a result of ill health, but later returned as a Lieutenant. Lieutenant D. W. Bizzell was promoted to Captain and given the company.

On June 9th Bragg ordered Forrest to attack the garrison at Triune, and determine, if possible, the intentions of the Federal right wing. The mission was carried out with the usual Forrest dash. Armstrong led the way on the Chapel Hill Pike and drove the Federal pickets pell-mell into the trench works in front of the town. The horse artillery was then brought up and a furious fire opened on the trenches and the town. While this fire fight was in progress, Forrest conducted his scouting mission and determined that the garrison was indeed a heavy one and that they were preparing for the road. At noon he broke off the action and retreated before the heavy infantry force sallying from the works.

Major Jeffrey Forrest, the General's brother, brought off a huge herd of cattle that had been destined for the Yankee cook pots and by late afternoon men and animals were safe behind the Harpeth.

Forrest's report to General Bragg that the Federals were preparing for action bore fruit on June 22nd. After much prodding from Washington and after much preparation, General Rosecrans moved south. Rosecrans was slow, methodical and skillful when goaded into action as Braxton Bragg was soon to learn. Swinging wide around Bragg's left below Triune, the Federals negated the heavy Confederate defensive system in front of Wartrace. On the 24th the Confederate Army was in full retreat towards the Tennessee. Rosecrans pressed them and pressed them hard. Knowing that Bragg would retreat into the impregnable fortress that was Chattanooga, Rosecrans planned to cross the Tennessee far to the west of the city, strike into Georgia behind Missionary Ridge and cut the railroads below Ringgold, thus rendering useless the Rebel works at Chattanooga. Rosecrans entertained vague hopes that, once in Bragg's rear below Chattanooga, Bragg would retreat all the way to Atlanta before holing up. All of his initial moves were successful beyond his expectations.

On the 24th, Rosecrans assailed the Confederates guarding the passes in Liberty and Bell Buckel Gaps, broke through and advanced on Tullahoma. Meanwhile, his cavalry columns under General D. S. Stanley hammered mercilessly at General Joe Wheeler's Rebels guarding the miles-long wagon train rumbling slowly forward through the mire. The rain had begun to fall late on the 23rd and was pouring in unremittent torrents into the day of the 26th. Wheeler's officers, knowing that the narrow bridge at Shelbyville over the now raging Duck River was the key to the escape of the army's wagons, fought the Federals with courage born of desperation. Stanley, just as aware as Wheeler of the importance of the bridge, attacked again and again attempting to break Wheeler's lines and cut the last avenue of escape of the wagon train.

The steady, desperate, mounted battles, scattered over the countryside, continued without letup until the late afternoon of the 27th, when the last wagon rolled across the bridge to temporary safety south of the Duck. An hour before sunset Wheeler gave up the village of Shelbyville to the Federal horsemen, withdrew his last vidette to the south bank and prepared to fire the bridge. Here occurred a rare and stirring incident of military courage and generosity at risk of life rarely equaled in history. Forrest, having been ordered to withdraw his pickets around Triune and join Wheeler in defense of the train, was riding hard through the pouring rain for the bridge at Shelbyville. One of his advance scouts arrived at the bridge just as Wheeler's men were setting it afire. Hearing that Forrest was approaching and fearing that he would be unaware that the Federals now held the town, Wheeler promptly acted. Taking immediate command of Martin's Division of some 500 men and 2 guns, Wheeler led them back across the bridge in the teeth of over-whelming numbers in a desperation move to hold the bridge for Forrest. In a smashing charge, the Federals were driven from the bridge face where Wheeler deployed his little force for action. He was barely in place when the determined Yankees in a close column of fours charged full speed down the main street of the town straight for the two cannon mounted on the bridge. The guns roared with double-shotted canister point-blank into the head of the column. A great number of men and horses went down in a welter of flying legs and tangled bodies, and the Federals had the guns. Close and desperate the conflict raged. Wheeler was soon aware that the cause was hopeless. The bridge was now under Federal control along with some five hundred yards of the bank and escape was cut off. Little Joe Wheeler ordered the "every-man-for-himself" command to be passed along and gathered about him a small group of his officers. Yelling to them, "Let's show them the way!", he wheeled his horse and charged straight for the river bank. Blasting a hole in the Federal line with their pistols, Wheeler led them up and over the bank. The river bank here was some twenty feet above the swollen stream but did not deter the determined Rebels. Sailing into empty air, the running horses landed nearly halfway across the river and sank below the surface of the muddy, surging torrent. Most of the horses and men surfaced, and like Wheeler and Martin, grasping the mane or tail of their swimming mounts, gained the opposite shore. Just under half the Confederate force remounted and escaped under a fusilade of fire from the Federal side. Half of Martin's men sank below the stream to rise no more under the shooting gallery practice or were captured and dragged from the river.

The wily Forrest, nearing the outskirts of Shelbyville, sent forward his trusty scouts and, upon learning of Wheeler's disaster, doubled back. Riding hard through the rain some five miles downstream from the bridge, he forced a crossing and at darkness his muddy and dripping command joined the rear of the floundering wagons.

On June 28th Forrest's command was assigned to picket the roads leading to Manchester and Hillsboro from Tullahoma. The next few days were given over to constant skirmishing with the slowly advancing columns of Rosecrans. In one of these many fights the gallant Colonel Starnes, one of Forrest's bravest men, was killed by a Federal sharpshooter. As Bragg continued his retreat to Chattanooga, Forrest was assigned the mission of protecting the rear of the army until it had passed the mountain gaps at Cowan. This mission he admirably performed at least in the eyes of General Bragg if not in the eyes of the local inhabitants. This doughty warrior enjoyed telling a story on himself of an incident at Cowan. Forrest said that as his men were slowly backing up the mountain, popping away at the advancing Federal horsemen, he, as the rear of his force, ran afoul an irate dame standing on her front porch. She screamed and shook her fist at him and he heard, (among other things), the words, "You great big cowardly rascal; why don't you turn and fight like a man instead of running like a cur? I wish old Forrest was here, he'd make you fight!" Forrest laughingly said that he had rather face an enemy battery than the aroused ire of that woman.

On the 4th of July, 1863 the Confederate Army under Braxton Bragg was safely ensconced in the fortress of Chattanooga. This day was to be the "Black Holiday" of the Confederacy. As Bragg had given up the State of Tennessee, never to recover it, so had General Pemberton given up the garrison of besieged Vicksburg. In addition to these disasters, the hitherto invincible Army of Robert E. Lee was stumbling southward from the uncalculable defeat at Gettysburg. These mighty blows of the Federal axe struck on the same day, eventually felled the Confederate Oak.

Chapter VII

CHICKAMAUGA

Following Bragg's retreat into the confines of Chattanooga, he dispersed his cavalry to watch for the certain advance of Rosecrans. Bragg was sure that Rosecrans would cross the Tennessee River above Chattanooga and swing wide around his right, coming down into North Georgia through the open country in that area. To this end he dispatched the troopers under Forrest to the upper reaches of the river near Kingston in East Tennessee. The Third Arkansas was assigned to the monotonous job of picketing the river near Rose's Mill in Meigs County.

Forrest had sent Colonel G. G. Dibrell and his Eighth Tennessee Regiment to Sparta earlier in the month to watch and report the advance of Rosecrans' Army. Dibrell's was a story in itself. He created great consternation in the enemy country. He whipped Union Colonel Minty's Brigade to a frazzle with his short-strength regiment of 300 men at Sparta and set off a chain reaction of letters and telegrams between the many and varied Federal Headquarters—"Where is Forrest?"—"Beware of Forrest!" —"Forrest is preparing to move into central Tennessee."—these and many more burned up the wires while Dibrell withdrew quietly and unobserved into Kingston.

While Forrest stole a march or two on the Federal Cavalry, General Rosecrans was stealing a big one on Braxton Bragg. Instead of striking for the rolling country east of Chattanooga as Bragg anticipated, Rosecrans, in a magnificent march, reached the fords down-stream from the city and by the 4th of September most of his army was over the river at Caperton's Ferry. Before Bragg was aware of the great danger involved in the enemy's move, Rosecrans men were pouring through the passes in Lookout Mountain and were force marching for North Georgia. Before the dilatant Bragg could make a decision, the Yankees made it for him. His sole course of action was a precipitate retreat down the railroad toward Ringgold and Dalton and even this became a foot-race since Rosecrans had a shorter distance to move. Chattanooga, the so-called "Impregnable Fortress" was abandoned without a shot being fired. Forrest was called in from east Tennessee to get between Bragg and the aggressive troopers of Rosecrans, and Wheeler was called in to guard the country near Rome. While the gray army gathered in the vicinity of Dalton and Lafayette, Forrest's men were pounding down the roads from Kingston. On September 6th, the gaunt horsemen rode through Bragg's Army and took position astride the Ringgold-Lafayette Road. At nightfall, Forest heard that General D. S. Stanley's crack mounted infantry had launched a foray against the railroad below Dalton and was backed by a brigade of infantry under General E. M. McCook. Speedy couriers rode throughout the night, tearing along the narrow dusty roads in the dark; and by 9 a. m. on the 8th, Forrest, Wheeler, Wharton and Martin were all arrayed against Stanley and were awaiting him in the narrow passes between Sand and Lookout Mountains. Stanley beat a hasty retreat—a wise decision. Before Stanley's dust had settled, Forrest was riding hard for Ringgold. His uncanny ability to outguess the enemy was never better demonstrated than in this series of rapid maneuvers.

Arriving at Ringgold on the night of the 10th, Forrest discovered that Crittenden's Federal Infantry Corps was moving in that direction, an act that would cut Bragg's Army nearly in half. At daylight on the 11th, Forrest tore into Crittenden's lead files. The Third Arkansas went in dismounted at a place called Confederate Hill. The resolute Confederate troopers held each rise in ground with great tenacity giving it up only when severely crowded by superior numbers. The regiment lost one man killed at Confederate Hill and one at Pea Vine Church. Six horses were also killed in this myriad of skirmishes. At Reaomi Church the aggressive Forrest petitioned Bragg to cut Crittenden off from the main Federal Army and finish him off. Bragg refused to move. During the next week of constant maneuvering, the Confederates lost opportunity after opportunity to separate and smash the divided wings of the Union Army as it blindly surged up and down the roads in front of Chickamauga Creek. At one time McCook's Corps was forty miles from Crittenden and General George H.

Thomas was twenty miles from McCook. Bragg made several half-hearted efforts to separate and smash the Federals; but, leaving the execution of the plans to subordinates, they failed. By the 17th Rosecrans was finally aware of his grave danger and was concentrating his army behind Chickamauga Creek on ground of his own choosing and awaiting Bragg's next move. Bragg, too, was aware of his failure to wreck his enemy while he had the opportunity, and was now moving rapidly to the front intending to fight him no matter what the circumstances.

In addition to the troops under Generals Polk, D. H. Hill, Buckner and W. H. T. Walker, Bragg was now reenforced with the magnificent infantry under General James Longstreet on loan from Robert E. Lee. With this force on September 18th, Bragg marched to Chickamauga. Approaching the creek, the Confederates presented a front nearly seven miles long. Forrest and his cavalry was on the extreme right above Reed's Bridge; Hood's Division of Longstreet's Corps next in line approaching the bridge; Walker marching to Alexander's Bridge in the center; Buckner's Division at Tedford's Ford; Polk approaching Lee and Gordon's Mill; D. H. Hill aiming for Crawfish Springs; and Wheeler's Cavalry on the extreme left. In this position they smashed across the creek and attacked.

By nightfall on the 18th the heavy skirmishing had developed the main battleline. While the Confederates slept, Rosecrans, now in a near state of panic, was sliding up the line to get nearer to Chattanooga. This action shifted the fight by two miles to the Confederate right as the battle opened on the 19th. Armstrong's Brigade was assigned to Polk's Corps as scouts and pickets, and saw but desultory fire on the 18th and 19th, but not so General Forrest with Pegram's Division of Cavalry on the right. A stern and bloody fight lasted all day with the dismounted horsemen clinging to every log and tree until physically dislodged by the blue infantry. Late in the day Forrest procured the infantry brigades of Generals Wilson, Walthall, Stovall and Ector and stabilized the front in that sector.

At nightfall the Third Arkansas, along with the balance of Armstrong's Brigade, arrived at Forrest's Headquarters. They were aligned in the darkness far to the right of General John C. Breckenridge who held the extreme right of the infantry line. The Third Arkansas, now without their horses, slept in line of battle. At daylight, Colonel Hobson had them up and ready. The attack was supposed to go forward at 7 a. m. but was delayed until 9:00 by tardiness in the issuance of rations. When it was ready the woods of Chickamauga erupted into an inferno of death unmatched in fury since the dawn of warfare. Breckenridge's Kentuckians and Govan's Arkansans threw themselves against the Federal works in a series of bloody charges that have little equal in history, while Cleburne and Hill smashed at the heavy trenches in Kelly's Fields.

Forrest swung his dismounted troopers around the far end of the line and turning south, swept the fields to his front. With the Third Arkansas in the first assault, Captain George W. Winburne of Company "G" was shot dead and Private J. P. Carrol fell at his side. As they swept onward, General D. H. Hill rode up to Forrest and told him that he had first taken his men for crack infantry because of their steadiness under fire and their steady advance. Forrest tipped his hat, thanked him and rode away.

The slaughter house on the right gained little ground against the stubborn defense of the Federals, but it did set the stage for the mighty victory that followed. Rosecrans panicked when Govan's Brigade of Arkansas Infantry and Forrest's Troopers reached his left rear causing him to send reenforcements from his key center to support his sagging left. General Longstreet, directing the attack on the Federal Center, saw this movement of troops and struck. The attack is probably one of the best timed and best executed maneuvers ever attempted in battle. The Confederates penetrated the hole in Rosecran's line, then swung to the right rolling the entire Federal Army back on itself. The men in blue gave up the field and fled in wild disorder toward safety in Chattanooga. Only General George Thomas stood his ground. His bloody defense of Snodgrass Hill is a great monument to the valor of the American fighting man. The Confederates spent the rest of the day demolishing Thomas' position and sealing a smashing victory for the Southern Army. Seventeen thousand Southerners lay in the reeking woods of Chickamauga as mute testimony to the ferocity of battle. The routed Federals left nearly as many behind in their demoralized flight toward Chattanooga.

Forrest lost no time in counting his losses or reckoning his laurels. At nightfall his weary troopers were back in the saddle following hard on the heels of the retreating Unionists.

As the first light of dawn broke over the hills below Missionary Ridge, Forrest with General Armstrong at his side was pressing toward Rossville when they came suddenly upon a regiment of Yankee horsemen blocking the road as rearguard to a vanishing infantry force. Without a second's hesitation, Forrest shouted to Armstrong, "Let's give them a dare!" The Third Arkansas riding in the van broke full stride behind Forrest and with a wild shout piled full speed into the waiting Federals. The fight was brief and vicious before the blue coats broke and fled. A wild shot fired in the confusion passed through the neck of the horse Forrest was riding severing the large artery in passage from which the blood spouted in a crimson fountain. The General leaned over, jammed his forefinger in the hole, held it there and charged on. When the last Federal had cleared the ridge, Forrest removed his finger and the horse sagged and died. This was only one of twenty-nine horses killed under Forrest during this war.

The pursuit of the Federals was carried at such speed that the lead fours rode under a platform built in a treetop still containing two Federal signalmen. Armstrong called them down, relieved them of their field glasses and he and Forrest were soon occupying this seat overlooking the Chattanooga valley. From this lofty perch he could see the city, the winding river, Lookout Mountain and all the country far to the north and east. Forrest then dictated his now famous dispatch to Bragg that should have sealed the doom of the Federal Army of Tennessee.

on the road
Sept 21st 1863

Genl
    We are in a mile of Rossville—have been on the point of Missionary Ridge and can see Chattanooga and everything around the Enemey's Trains are leaving going around the point of Lookout Mountain—

    The Prisoners captured report two pontoons thrown across for the purpose of retreating I think they are evacuating as hard as they can go—

    They are cutting timber down to obstruct our passage

    I think we ought to push forward as rapidly as possible

Respectfully yr

N. B. Forrest
Brig Gen

Lt. Gen Polk
Please forward to Gen Bragg

The original document is badly scribbled in places which the officers present attributed to a horse stomping and shaking to move biting flies while his saddle skirt was being used as a writing table by Forrest's Adjutant. The information contained in the dispatch was never acted upon. Controversy raged over the years as to why Bragg did not immediately march on Chattanooga and follow the demoralized Federals through Tennessee. No satisfactory answer has ever been presented. In any case, Bragg's failure to act after Chickamauga was a major factor in the final outcome of the war. Certainly Forrest had some hard things to say about the affair as subsequent events were to demonstrate. By the time the Confederates moved to the crest of Lookout Mountain and Missionary Ridge on the 24th, Chattanooga was once again a formidable fortress far beyond any hope of being taken by assault. Forrest's Cavalry was relieved by the infantry and sent to Byrd's Mill to shoe the horses and refit after many hard months of campaigning. The Third Arkansas had come off lucky from the fiery furnace of Chickamauga. Despite being in the heat of the second day's battle they had lost only four men. Captain Winburne and Private Carroll were killed and Privates J. N. Organ and Silas Magby were wounded. Lieutenant Jeremiah Dumas was promoted to Captain of Company "K" replacing Winburne and the regiment went back to the war.

On September 25th news reached General Bragg that Federal General Ambrose Burnside's Army had reached Harrison, Tennessee en route from Knoxville to Chattanooga. He sent Forrest to intercept them and report on their intentions. By late afternoon the gray horsemen were on the move. As they passed through Chickamauga Station a courier caught up with Forrest and handed him a dispatch ordering him to proceed at once to Charleston by way of Cleveland, intercept a heavy force of cavalry at that point and drive them across the Hiawassee River. Arriving at Charleston at daylight the following morning, Forrest could see a heavy force of cavalry, preparing to ford, coming in his direction. In his usual fashion he struck first. Bringing his artillery up at a gallop and unlimbering in full view of the enemy, he went into action. While the cannon blasted away at the Federals, Forrest routed Dibrell's men around a point of land to the right while Armstrong moved right across in the enemy's front. In less than a half hour the entire command was over the river and pursuing the retreating Federals. At Philadelphia the blue coats attempted a stand, but Armstrong's Brigade, coming on at a gallop, charged into them driving them in full flight from the field. In the horse race that followed the Arkansans and Texans had capitol pistol practice for a few miles up the narrow roads. When the smoke blew away there were a hundred and twenty Federal prisoners in the bag and twenty-two to be buried.

The Third Arkansas paid a price for their position in the

front. Captain A. B. Duke of Company "K" now consolidated with old Company "C," was grieviously wounded in the hip by a shell splinter and was out of the war. Lieutenant Joseph Cole was promoted to Captain to fill this vacancy. In addition to Duke the Organ brothers, Tom and John, both were shot from their saddles, seriously wounded. Another strange coincidence of war.

On the 27th, 28th and 29th the command picketed the river and recovered from the hard march up from Chattanooga. On the morning of September 30th, the axe of fate fell. A courier arrived in the camps from Bragg's Headquarters with the following dispatch for Forrest:

Missionary Ridge, September 28th 1863

Brigadier General Forrest, near Athens:

General—The General Commanding desires that you will without delay turn over the troops of your command, previously ordered, to Major General Wheeler.

This petty act of personal vengeance against the best cavalry combat commander in the Confederacy, made with disregard for the good of the cause, provoked the precise response to be expected from such an act. Nathan Forrest flew into a towering rage and wrote Bragg a letter while his blood was at fever pitch. Among other things he accused Bragg of duplicity and lying and said he would soon call at his headquarters and repeat personally what he had written. A few days later, accompanied by Dr. J. B. Cowan, Forrest arrived at Bragg's tent and did precisely what he had said he was going to do. Dr. Cowan described the encounter by saying that Bragg offered his hand to Forrest who refused it and while jabbing his forefinger under Bragg's nose let go the following barrage of enraged language.

"I am not here to pass civilities or compliments with you, but on other business. You commenced your cowardly and contemptible persecution of me soon after the Battle of Shiloh, and you have kept it up ever since. You did it because I reported to Richmond facts, while you reported damned lies. You robbed me of my command in Kentucky, and gave it to one of your favorites men that I armed and equipped from the enemies of our country. In a spirit of revenge and spite, because I would not fawn upon you as others did, you drove me into west Tennessee in the winter of 1862, with a second brigade I had organized, with improper arms and without sufficient ammunition, although I had made repeated applications for the same. You did it to ruin me and my career. When in spite of all this I returned with my command, well equipped by captures, you began again your work of spite and persecution, and have kept it up; and now this second brigade, organized and equipped without thanks to you or the government, a brigade which has won a reputation for successful fighting second to none in the army, taking advantage of your position as the commanding general in order to further humiliate me, you have taken these brave men from me.

"I have stood your meanness as long as I intend to. You have played the part of a damned scoundrel, and are a coward, and if you were any part of a man I would slap your jaws and force you to resent it. You may as well not issue any more orders to me, for I will not obey them, and I will hold you personally responsible for any further indignities you endeavor to inflict upon me. You have threatened to arrest me for not obeying your orders promptly. I dare you to do it, and I say to you that if you ever again try to interfere with me or cross my path it will be at the peril of your life."

Forrest's later prediction to Dr. Cowan that Bragg would not utter one word nor make any charges concerning the incident proved correct. This brilliant combat officer accompanied only by a small staff rode westward into Mississippi there to recruit a new command and produce even greater military miracles.

In the camps near Athens, Tennessee the embittered horsemen now had a new commander in the person of Lieutenant General Joseph Wheeler. Wheeler was a man small in stature but large in courage. He was five feet three inches tall and weighed one hundred and fifteen pounds. This combination of a little man with unquestionable courage and love of battle had earned him the sobriquet of "The War Child." The Third Arkansas, then, along with the balance of Forrest's men, were now in their words, "The War Child's Children."

Chapter VIII

RAID

With the advent of Wheeler and the amalgamation of the two commands, it was the consensus of the officers that action was in the offing. They were not long in learning the facts. Wheeler had been ordered by Bragg to assume command of all the cavalry in the district, cross Walden's Ridge, interrupt the Federal supply line to beleaguered Chattanooga, and wreak general havoc in central Tennessee.

Following the Battle of Chickamauga the beaten Federals had holed up in the city where they were now trapped by the Rebels, and were slowly being reduced to near starvation. It was Bragg's intention to cut off their last channel of support on the wagon trails between the railheads at Nashville and the opposite bank of the Tennessee River at Chattanooga.

At this point in the story of the Third Arkansas Cavalry, an interesting personal story appears. The morning report for Company "D" indicates that Captain Thomas C. DeCaulp "deserted his country and went over to the enemy this date," (September 21, 1863). While searching through the Official Records at the National Archives, a letter was discovered from a United States Senator to "The Commander, Minnesota Department, U. S. Army." The letter said in part that it was to introduce a young soldier of fine merit who would enlist in the command under an assumed name, (his real name must be kept secret). The Senator explained that the man in reality was Thomas C. DeCaulp of Arkansas who had been "forced into the Rebel Service and was from the beginning a good Union man." The Senator did mention that DeCaulp had risen to Captain in the Rebel Cavalry

Service, but failed to mention that DeCaulp must have been a pretty fair Rebel soldier to rise to Captain despite his handicap of "being a good Union Man." Lieutenant William J. Bass was promoted to replace DeCaulp.

The new Commanding General lost not a moment. On the 29th of September, the day of his arrival, he completed his organization. The sick, the wounded and the weak were weeded out, horse and man. Brigadier General Frank C. Armstrong pleaded ill and refused to go. No one doubted that his love for Forrest and his detestation of Wheeler prompted his illness. The members of Forrest's old command would never forget Wheeler's mismanaged disaster in his effort to retake Fort Donelson on February 3rd, 1863. The final organization consisted of Brigadier General H. B. Davidson's Division with Colonels George B. Hodge's and J. L. Scott's Brigades; Brigadier General William T. Martin's Division with Colonel's John T. Morgan and A. A. Russell's Brigades; Brigadier General John A. Wharton's Division consisting of Colonels C. C. Crews' and Thomas Harrison's Brigades. The Third Arkansas Regiment was assigned to Russell's Brigade of Martin's Division. The artillery for this enterprise was the famous Arkansas Battery of Horse Artillery under Captain J. H. Wiggins.

At nightfall they moved forward to the Tennessee River opposite Cotton Port and encamped. Shortly after daylight Wiggins galloped his battery into action and opened fire on the Fourth Ohio guarding the opposite bank while Morgan's Brigade dashed across the shallow river scattering the Federals to the hills. By noon the entire command was over the river. Riding hard on through the night, the base of Walden's Ridge was reached early on October 1st. Here a long halt was called to feed and rest the horses and allow the men a brief respite. Pushing forward again after noon, the long grueling climb up Walden's Ridge began. It was past midnight when the exhausted horses topped this towering mass of rock and trees and started downhill to Sequatchie Valley.

Shortly before dawn, another rest halt was called to recoup men and animals before debouching onto the valley floor. At 8 a. m. the now rested command was back in the saddle with Martin's Division up front and pushing rapidly for Anderson's Crossroads at the main Sequatchie Valley Pike.

Here occurred one of the rare turns in the fortunes of war. As the advance guard under Colonel Morgan approached the crossroad where vision was unobstructed by the hills, they were confronted by the sight of an enormous wagon train ten miles long stretching away through the valley. At this time, too, they rode pointblank into the infantry escort for the wagons. Without stopping to consider the odds, Morgan charged. The Federal Infantry stood their ground and Morgan was driven back. Russell's Brigade now rode on the scene. Rapidly swinging the Third Arkansas, First Confederate and Fourth Alabama into line, Russell, now joined by Morgan, charged into the fray. In a matter of minutes the entire infantry escort threw down their arms and surrendered. Then ensued a scene of panic and motion beyond the scope of the best imagination. Thirteen hundred wagons, pulled by 5,200 mules broke full speed down the narrow road. Yankee teamsters standing in the seats lashing on their frantic beasts, yelling, cursing and laying on the whips; clouds of dust boiling off the sun-parched roads; streams of Rebel Cavalrymen spewing down out of the hills riding at racing speed parallel to the train, blazing away at pointblank range into men and mules. Wagon after wagon spilled over into the road jamming the ones following behind. In a matter of minutes the entire panic-stricken convoy had been brought to a halt.

Wheeler, knowing that time was now on the side of the enemy, quickly got control of the command and the systematic destruction of the train was begun. The mules were sabered in the traces to conserve ammunition and the wagons were put to the torch. The prisoners were lined up and paroled; and in less than eight hours, the Rebel column was pounding northward toward McMinnville. The work was completed none too soon. Colonel E. M. McCook's Federal Cavalry Brigade appeared on the scene just as Wheeler was pulling out. Wharton's Division was detailed to fend him off until the raiders were well on their way northward. Through several hours and many miles the steady rumble of exploding ammunition in the burning wagons was heard by the fast moving raiders. In one stroke and a chance of fate, irreparable harm was done to the Federals penned up in Chattanooga, already desperately short of food and ammunition. Thirteen hundred wagons, 5,200 mules and hundreds of tons of food and ammunition had gone up in smoke.

At noon on October the 4th, Hodge's Brigade of Davidson's Division now in the advance appeared before the outskirts of McMinnville. He promptly divided his command, routing one column to the north and one to the west of the town effectively blocking the avenues of escape for the Federal Garrison. Wharton's Division coming on next completed the envelopment. Wharton then sent Hodge into the town under a flag of truce to demand the prompt and unconditional surrender of the garrison. Major M. L. Patterson, with his Fourth Tennessee (Federal Infantry) lost no time making up his mind. His 600 man garrison marched out and laid down their arms. It was a fine haul. An entire railroad train loaded with food and clothing was found on a siding and many warehouses in the town were bulging with stores of various kinds. A full day and a night were occupied in the burning of the train, stores, depot and a rail bridge over Hickory Creek. In addition 200 fine horses were appropriated for the command.

Here also the first indication of General Wheeler's notorious inability to maintain discipline in his command became apparent. This fault was to plague him till the end of the war, sometimes over-shadowing his brilliant record as a combat soldier. The Federal Commander later complained that when his men were lined up for paroling the Rebel horsemen indiscriminately relieved them of boots, watches, wallets and whatever else they could find of value. He said he complained to a Confederate Captain that he would report the matter to General Wheeler who was now in the town. He said the Captain told him he could report anything he wished and it would do him no good since "Joe Wheeler couldn't make them do a damn thing they didn't want to do." The Captain must have been fairly sure of his ground since obviously nothing was done or said about it.

By 3 p. m. the command was back in the saddle headed northward through Clearmont, Woodbury and on to Readyville. By now, too, the Federal hornet's nest was aroused. Brigadier General George Crook's Division of Federal Cavalry headed by Wilder's famous mounted infantry brigade had been pounding up the road from Sequatchie Valley. Between Clearmont and Woodbury they charged into the rearguard under General Martin causing the entire column to be halted and moved into battle line. A nasty little skirmish was fought before the Federals were driven off. In addition to Crook, General David Stanley's crack Federal Division was closing in from the north and east. Long after nightfall when the Federals were encamped, Wheeler was urging on the tired column of Rebel Raiders. Shortly after daylight on the 5th of October, Wheeler appeared before Murphreesboro. Knowing from past experience that Murphreesboro was an entrenched camp, Wheeler simply created a heavy diversion. Dis-

Federal stockade guarding Murfreesboro railroad bridge

McMinnville railroad bridge smashed by Wheeler's Raiders

mounting Davidson's Division, they were sent forward on foot to bring heavy fire on the town's defenders. While this noisy show was in progress, Martin and Wharton's Division were routed around the town to the rail bridge and railroad. The north end of the bridge was guarded by a fifty-two man garrison ensconced in a heavy log stockade. Wheeler brought up Wiggin's Battery and ordered him to throw a few shells through the fort. With his usual efficiency, Wiggins was soon throwing clouds of logs and splinters. In short order, the white flag was flown and the garrison marched out and surrendered. The vital railroad bridge was promptly burned and three miles of track were torn up and warped beyond use by heating the rails on piles of burning cross-ties.

As soon as the destruction was complete, Wheeler called in the command, remounted and swung wide to the west of the town. As the now nearly exhausted command moved out, Wheeler's scouts reported that Crook was coming hard on his heels and was only a few hours behind. Stanley's Division was closing from the north effectively blocking all movement to the north and west. With the receipt of this information the "War Child" became a little apprehensive. Realizing that he was leaving a trail too broad and too wide and that every hour that passed was bringing his command nearer to disaster, he decided on a diversion. Colonel A. A. Russell's Brigade, the best in the command, was selected for the mission. Russell's orders were to cut into the main road towards Franklin and move rapidly in that direction. He was told to get as near to Franklin as possible drawing as many of the Federals behind him as was safe; but, when too hard pressed, to turn southward cross-country for the Duck River, cross at White's Bridge and rejoin the command somewhere enroute to Pulaski. This order was promptly placed in execution.

Stringing out into a column of fours they headed northwestward at a gallop. Colonel Hobson had the point with the Third Arkansas, the Fourth Alabama next in line, the First Confederate bringing up the rear. The head of Stanley's column was struck fifteen miles from Murphreesboro. Russell's quick sweeping look showed only one regiment in the main road and the rest of the Federal column strung out for miles along a side road leading to Triune. Russell never slackened the pace. Turning to Colonel Hobson he yelled, "Charge 'em, Hobson!" Before the surprised Federals could gather their wits, the Arkansans bore down on them at full gallop. The wild screech of the Rebel Yell, rumble of hooves and the exploding crackle of pistol fire were on them before they could raise their guns. The Federals were literally blown off the road. Continuing straight on at a dead run, the rearguard shot their way through what was left of the opposition and swept on towards Franklin. Russell did not call a halt to blow the horses until ten miles past the collision point. The First Confederate was dismounted and deployed across the roads to stand off the pursuing enemy until the exhausted horses could recover sufficiently to move on.

Russell called a hurried conference of his three regimental commanders to discuss the degree of execution of Wheeler's orders. There was no doubt that Stanley's entire division had been diverted from their purpose of attacking the main column, since this overwhelming force was now rapidly closing in to finish off this little brigade of Rebel Raiders. Russell's orders were to move out cross-country. They would turn south and west, keeping to bridlepaths and lesser roads until they could intercept the main road leading from Franklin to White's Bridge on the Duck. Hobson was ordered to replace the First Confederate as rearguard, remaining mounted giving the First Confederate time to reach their horses, remount and follow the Fourth Alabama out.

Hobson commanded the regiment to mount up, form fours and move out. As the head of the regiment approached the position of the First Confederate they met them moving slowly backward down the brushy slope toward the creek bottom where the regiment had halted. They were being hard pressed. The steady splatter of rifle shots echoed down the hill as Stanley's leading unit advanced steadily against the outnumbered gray coats. Hobson instantly saw that a shock tactic was necessary to give the First Confederate time to reach their horses and mount. He shouted to an officer passing by on foot to make for their horses and follow the Fourth Alabama. Then, drawing his sword, he yelled, "Forward at the gallop—Ho-o!" As soon as the column was well in motion his next command echoed down the files, "Draw pistols— CHARGE!" At full gallop the Arkansans rode over the front line of dismounted Federal Cavalrymen. Firing into them point-blank with their revolvers, they topped the rise at full speed and rode head on into the mounted column following up the dismounted troopers. A wild melee of slashing sabers, and blazing pistols followed. The Federal Column was doubled back on itself in the road creating terrific confusion in the Yankee ranks. In one of the rare freaks of close combat not a man in the Third Arkansas was hit though there were many emptied saddles on the other side. Hobson, keeping a cool head throughout, seeing that the necessary shock had been accomplished, ordered the regiment cut. Doubling back on the narrow road was difficult and dangerous, and soon degenerated into every man for himself. They had to ride out the same way they rode in—back through the scattered Yankee troopers on foot. Through a wild fusilade of shots, they passed over the ridge and down into the valley out of range. They came off unscathed and rode southward in Russell's tracks.

Far into the night the weary troopers pushed on following on the heels of the rest of Russell's Brigade. No halt was called until 2 a. m. when the now benumbed raiders were allowed three hours of rest, sleeping in the road, bridle reins of the horses looped around their arms. Shortly before daylight they were back in the saddle and pushing southward. Around noon the dusty column of twos entered the main road leading to White's Bridge.

The rear of the column had just moved into the road when their bluecoated pursuers hove into view. Colonel Hobson ordered them forward with all the speed they could make, but it wasn't enough. The Federals charged into the rear of the Arkansans just as they reached the bridge. In the hilt-to-hilt encounter that followed, Privates Ed Toms and Sam Blumenthal were sabered from their sadles and left behind. To the everlasting gratitude of the Third Arkansas, Colonel Russell was waiting for them at the bridge. He allowed the weary Arkansans to pass through, then assailed the head of the Yankee column. This action effectively stalled further pursuit and the brigade moved on in the direction of Farmington.

While Russell was absent, Wheeler's Raiders had been busy people. On the 6th of October, while Wharton's Division fended off Crook's persistent Federals, Davidson and Martin had played havoc with the Yankee supply system. At Christianna and Fosterville two complete trains were captured and burned. Every railroad bridge between Murphreesboro and Wartrace had been laid in ruins. Late in the afternoon Wheeler with Davidson's Division entered Shelbyville where huge quantities of stores were found. They were put to the torch and the command moved on to near Warner's Bridge on the Duck. By now the Confederate command had reached a stage of near demoralization. Days and nights of riding, fighting and working without sleep had taken its toll. Wheeler had too long delayed in the area and was now securely trapped between the jaws of the Federal pincers that were about to slam shut. In addition, heavy forces of Federal Infantry were coming by forced marches in an effort to cut off his last line of retreat across the Tennessee.

After dark on the 6th Wheeler issued his orders for placement of his divisions. Even to this day, with time to study, it is impossible to understand what these orders were. Davidson was to camp at Warner's Bridge; Martin's two miles below; and Wharton's two miles below Martin. Davidson was told that if they were attacked he was to move towards Wharton for greater numbers. At daylight it happened. Crook attacked in force. Wheeler now ordered Davidson to move southward toward Crowell's Mill. Davidson, however, obeyed the first order and moved toward Farmington. This opened a gap between Davidson and Wharton into which Crook's leading division moved. When Wheeler reached the outskirts of Farmington with Martin, Davidson was already being belabored by half of Crook's Division. Wheeler charged into the fray, attempting to form Davidson's men into a column of fours with Martin's Division in line, but it didn't work. Crook was not to be denied his prize. Wilder's mounted troopers charged full tilt into Davidson's demoralized men, smashing them back on Martin's half formed line where both divisions broke in panic and fled.

Meantime, west of Farmington, the balance of Crook's Division debouched into the main road in Wheeler's rear cutting off Russell's Brigade that was now approaching the field. General George B. Hodge, in his report, obviously tearfully written, says that he saw Scott's panic-stricken brigade bearing down on him at "racing speed." Hodge's horse was knocked from under him and both fell sprawling into a field which undoubtedly saved his life. He said he made desperate efforts to reform his men and check the pursuit of the enemy. He got part of them into line where he said he fought a raging battle for five hours over seventeen miles of ground being continually battered, shelled and charged. His plaintive report ended with "my gallant brigade was cut to pieces and slaughtered."

Russell's little brigade never reached the main force fighting in Farmington. In a terrific charge the Third Arkansas, Fourth Alabama and First Confederate literally cut their way through the Federal Legions in order to join the panicked flight of Wheeler's demoralized command. The Third Arkansas left behind Privates Childers, Thomas, and Parham who had been cut from their saddles and captured.

It wasn't until the disordered command reached Shelbyville that Wheeler could bring some semblance of order into the Rebel Command. Here late on the 8th, Wharton's Division was detailed as rearguard with orders to delay their pursuers long enough to give the rest of the command time to reach the fords on the Tennessee at Mussel Shoals. The relentless Wilder was not to be checked. His Seventeenth and Ninety-eighth Indiana battered down Martin's feeble barricades totally routing the defenders and driving them to the woods. With disaster on their heels the Rebel Raiders, now solely concerned with individual safety, were making the greatest possible speed toward the Tennessee.

Through Pulaski to Rogersville the weary horses stumbled on. At Rogersville the command turned left on the Athens Road then cut cross-country to Watkin's Farm on the banks of the river. Here Wheeler detailed Morgan's Brigade of Russell's Division to make a last stand in order to give his disordered command time to ford the shallow but fast running Tennessee. They were hardly in place before the head of the Federal column appeared. A hot fire fight occurred and the stubborn Rebels held their ground. When the last of the wagons and ambulances were over, Morgan ordered the Fourth Alabama and Third Arkansas to mount up and be last to cross. Just at sunset when the rear of the Confederate column was nearly to the water's edge, the Fifth Iowa bore down on them at full speed, sabers drawn, in a column of fours. Colonel Russell wheeled his two regiments around and counter-charged. A wild close quarter fight developed in which the Iowans were driven back to Watkin's Farm. The Rebels then crossed unmolested to safety beyond the Tennessee. In this last fracas the Third Arkansas left Privates R. T. Crowson and A. D. LeCroy wounded and in the hands of the foe.

Wheeler would not allow the weary command to halt or rest until he had pushed them on to Courtland far down the railroad east of Tuscumbia. Here at last a halt was called and camp was made. The raid into Tennessee had in a large sense been highly successful. Tens of millions of dollars worth of supplies and equipment had been destroyed. Nearly a hundred miles of railroad track and four railroad bridges had been wrecked. The Sequatchie Valley wagon train capture was in itself nearly full payment for the cost of the raid. On the dark side, Wheeler's management of his command left much to be desired and demonstrated again his historical unwillingness or inability to maintain discipline in the command.

Shortly after reaching permanent camp Major J. F. Earle resigned and returned to Arkansas and Captain William H. Blackwell of Company "B" was promoted to Major in his stead. Lieutenant John F. Lindell was promoted to Captain replacing Blackwell.

Chapter IX

Eleven days were spent in the quiet of the camps at Courtland. Here the command rested, re-fitted and regained the spirit lost in the disaster at Farmington. Here, too, the bandy-legged little General Joe Wheeler met the woman who was later to become his wife. His courtship was all too brief. On October 20th, "boots and saddles" was heard in the camp and the command moved out of Courtland bound for Missionary Ridge at Chattanooga. A long weary march was made over the sand hills and mountains of North Alabama ending on the old battlefield at Chickamauga on the 31st of October.

Here at Chickamauga Station Wheeler was ordered to reform the command and reorganize the cavalry corps to encompass the independent brigades operating with the Army of Tennessee. The final organization was made up of two divisions under Major General William T. Martin and Brigadier General Frank C. Armstrong. Martin's Division consisted of the brigades of Brigadier General John T. Morgan and Colonel C. C. Crews. Armstrong's Division comprised the brigades of Colonel Thomas Harrison and Colonel George Dibrell. Harrison had been a Captain in the gallant old Eighth Texas when it was first organized out of the Texas Rangers. This great association created a first class cavalry brigade. The Third Arkansas was assigned to this crack unit, their companion regiments being the Eighth Texas and the Eleventh Texas.

Following the unexplainable reluctance of Bragg to follow up his mighty victory at Chickamauga, the Confederates had occupied the high range of hills in front of Chattanooga including

Missionary Ridge and Lookout Mountain. The penned in Federals had been reduced to near starvation until the night of October 28th. On this day Hooker's XI and XII Corps forced a crossing at Brown's Ferry and at the Battle of Wauhatchie Station routed Longstreet's Command and opened the river to navigation. The one steamship available to the Federals, later known as the "Cracker Line," brought in food and forage to put new life into the cornered Federals. This failure by Longstreet was mainly a result of the dissatisfaction and demoralization within Bragg's Command. President Davis visited the camps in a personal attempt to investigate and solve the difficulties between Braxton Bragg and his generals. Davis' personal regard for Bragg overrode every military consideration despite testimony from every senior officer in the command that Bragg was incompetent and unable to maintain discipline and cohesion. The result was that Bragg was left in command, several top generals were transferred and Longstreet was ordered into east Tennessee to assail and capture the Federal IX Corps under General Ambrose Burnside. Burnside had occupied east Tennessee including the city of Knoxville and was at this moment moving westward toward Chattanooga to relieve the siege of that place.

There was bitter animosity between Longstreet and Bragg, thus it was with mutual satisfaction that Longstreet marched away from Missionary Ridge on November 5th bound for east Tennessee. Wheeler's entire cavalry command was ordered to report to Longstreet and assist him in the march to Knoxville and the campaign against Burnside.

On November 6th, Longstreet's columns were well on their way toward Cleveland and Sweetwater. On the 11th Wheeler was ordered to ride on to Maryville and capture the garrison at that place then picket the river northward. On November 12th, 1863, the campaign of east Tennessee opened with a bang.

Wheeler reached the Little Tennessee River at Motley's Ford near noon and was faced with the Eleventh Kentucky guarding the opposite bank. Captain Wiggins' ever faithful battery galloped up to the water's edge, unlimbered in full view of the Federals and opened fire. While his shells fell thick and fast among the blueclad horsemen, Dibrell's Brigade splashed into the river and plunged across. With a whoop and cry the Tennesseeans charged into the Kentuckians. The Federals attempted to stand but the fast firing six shooters in the hands of the determined Rebels broke them. In full flight the Federals ran with Dibrell in hot pursuit. One hundred and fifty-one of them were knocked from their horses and captured. The balance of Wheeler's Command now crossed and followed hard on the heels of Dibrell's men.

Armstrong, riding at the head of Harrison's Brigade, was pounding up the road when suddenly Dibrell's column came back at full speed with the full Kentucky Brigade under Colonel Frank Wolford close on their heels. There was no time to deploy. Drawing his sword he screamed out, "CHARGE!" and clapped the spurs to his mount. The Arkansans and Texans rode full tilt into the heard of the Kentucky column smashing them back on the rear regiments. The fight was in full swing when Morgan's Brigade of Martin's Division charged into the fray. The Rebel weight was too much. The Kentuckians broke and fled, the yelling Rebels pounding at their heels. Through Maryville and on to the Little River, the horse race went on. Another eighty-five Kentuckians were captured and twenty-two killed in the wild pursuit.

By the time all of Wheeler's Command had closed to the river, the sun was going down so the pursuit was called off and the weary troopers went into camp. At daylight Wheeler put the command across the river. This time he was faced by an entire Federal Cavalry Division under Brigadier General James Shackelford. The "War Child" was not to be deterred. Both divisions were thrown in and the Federals were driven some seven miles cross-country to Stock Creek. Here the blue coats held up. A line of hills beyond the creek was occupied in force and the bridge was burned. Immediately on reaching the creek, Wheeler deployed for action. Martin's Division was dismounted, the held horses taken to the rear and the men routed downstream to turn the Federal right. While the dismounted men were wading the stream, the balance of the command was put in place. The formation was powerful. Harrison was formed with regiments in line; the ever faithful Eighth Texas in front, Eleventh Texas in the center and the Third Arkansas in the rear. Dibrell's Brigade was formed in a column of fours and followed in support.

When Martin's men struck the Federal right full in flank, the confused Yankees gave way and began drawing back on their center. Wheeler was waiting for this precise moment. Standing high in the stirrups the fighting little bantam shouted out, "Forward at a gallop—HO-O!" As soon as the first lines were across the shallow run his high-pitched voice sliced through the rumble of hooves, "CHARGE!" With a wild yell of the mountain fox hunters, the Rebels bore down on the addled Federals at racing speed. Up and over the hasty barricade they poured, pistols blazing. The Kentuckians dissolved and scattered. It was every man for himself in a confused chase across the countryside. Over ten miles of fences, hedges and ditch banks, the Kentuckians raced for the pontoon bridge at Knoxville and expected safety inside the Federal lines. Hard on their heels, the Texans and Arkansans shot and slashed them out of the saddles. The chase didn't end until the pontoon bridge was in sight. By this time one hundred and forty Federals were in the bag and another fifty-two were killed. The Kentucky Brigade was nearly destroyed. Wheeler's loss in the entire march was trifling. In the Third Arkansas not a man was wounded seriously enough to put him out of action. It had been a one-sided fight. The willingness of the Rebel Cavalrymen to close with the enemy and the fierceness of his charge was still paying off.

Longstreet's Infantry was now approaching Campbell's Station on the Tennessee and Georgia Railroad some twenty miles from Knoxville and needed his cavalry to guard his approaches. On the 17th, the cavalry command crossed the Holston and established the siege lines. Wheeler spread a thin line from the Holston on the right to the Clinton and Knoxville Railroad on the left. In this position he awaited Longstreet's arrival. When the foot-sore infantrymen filed into the trenches, Wheeler slipped to the left occupying the last half-mile. Here for six days the dismayed horsemen crouched in the trenches listening to the screech and boom of artillery shells that fell constantly in the area. The Federals, holed up in the town, meant to make a fight of it—and did as subsequent events were to prove.

On November 22nd Wheeler was ordered to withdraw his horsemen from the trenches, move to Kingston and clean out the Federal garrison at that place. Kingston was fifty miles away and in the rear of the Rebel Army, and Longstreet felt that they had to be eliminated. At daylight on the 23rd the command was on the road. Winter had now set in in the Tennessee Mountains. It was bitter cold and a mixture of freezing rain and snow was falling. Clothing was in bad shape in the Confederate Cavalry. Blankets were in short supply and heavy coats were a rare thing indeed. Despite these handicaps, the hurrying column made twenty-six miles over the miserable mountain roads and made a freezing bivouac. On the 24th another twenty-four miles were covered and at sunset the command appeared before the town.

The Yankee garrison of Kingston was no milk sop. Wheeler lost no time going into action. Martin's Division was dismounted and sent in. Armstrong's Division followed in support, mounted. The rumble of battle was sudden and final. In less than an hour Wheeler could see that he was not going to take this town. A heavy garrison of both infantry and cavalry held extensive trench works well studded with artillery and they fought back with confidence and skill. As soon as total darkness fell, Wheeler called off the action and withdrew quietly up the Knoxville Road. Three days later the half frozen horsemen were back with the main army.

On the 28th they crossed over the Holston and chased off a force of Federal foragers and picketed the upper reaches of the river. On this date General Wheeler was recalled to the Army of Tennessee to regroup the cavalry following Bragg's disastrous defeat at the hands of Grant. Also Longstreet made his long postponed attack on Knoxville which resulted in a murderous repulse and failure. It was a bad week for the Confederacy. General Martin moved up to take Wheeler's place and General J. T. Morgan moved up to division command. Colonel A. A. Russell of the Fourth Alabama was given command of Morgan's Brigade.

At sunset the command was ordered back across the Holston and directed to march in the direction of Tazewell to meet a Federal column approaching from that direction.

November 29th was a hard day. The road was rough, the hills were high and the weather was biting cold. By the time the command approached the village of Maynardsville, several men had their feet frozen in the stirrups. As they entered the valley of Bull Run Creek, the steady popping of skirmish fire reached their ears from the direction of the town. This action was between Brigadier General William E. "Grumble" Jones and his Virginia troopers from Major General Robert Ransom's Division of southwest Virginia and the relieving column of Federals coming from Kentucky by way of Cumberland Gap. Jones was retreating before this heavy force but was fighting them through every yard.

A hurried conference between Martin and Jones was held in the road and a plan was agreed upon whereby Martin would move cross-country to the right coming into the road between Head of Barren and Rutledge, then double back taking the Federals in rear. Leaving Jones to hold the front at Maynardsville, Martin's troopers cut down the valley floor. Within an hour darkness fell. A terrible night was spent slipping and sliding on the icy roads.

Several men and horses were seriously injured by falling from the ledges into the rocky creek bottoms. At daylight the shivering, freezing Rebels entered the Rutledge Road. Turning left, Martin urged on the suffering troops. By 11 a. m. a wan sun and hurrying beasts had warmed up the command and at 1 p. m. the Yankees appeared. Somehow the Federals had been apprised of their danger and were withdrawing toward the Clinch River Crossing below Head of Barren.

Quickly throwing the Brigades of Russell and Harrison into line, Martin ordered the charge. With a yell they lunged forward. A rocky field full of scrub cedar trees was crossed at full gallop and they piled into the Federals on the narrow road. The blue coats made no effort to stand. They broke for the Clinch River at full speed Harrison's Brigade riding down their rear. The narrowness of the road which suddenly entered a steep gorge saved the Federals from total disaster. The Confederate line slowly squeezed into a column of twos as the pounding horses entered the gorge. The rear of the Yankee column was all that was available to the onrushing graybacks and they picked them off one at a time.

The Clinch was crossed through floating ice at 4 p. m. and the Federals driven almost into the town of Head of Barren by nightfall. When a halt was called after dark the exhausted Rebels had to break ice clubs to free the tails of their mounts. Icicles hung from the horses' bellies to the ground and the lower legs of the men were encased in rock hard sheets of ice. Some coffee was discovered in a captured supply wagon overturned in one of the steep gorges and was the first the Confederates had seen in four months. Steaming pots of this beverage and roaring fires soon added a degree of comfort in the sinking cold night.

At daylight it was "Boots and Saddles" and back across the icy Clinch. Jones was left to guard the passes on the Rutledge Road and Martin moved on back to Knoxville to report to Longstreet for new fields of duty.

The wild race down the steep gorges and the melee during the Clinch crossing had not been a free ride. Lieutenants Francis A. Hobson and Marion E. Davis were seriously wounded; and two privates, Robert Rice and Robert Rae were buried in the lonely, ice clogged bottoms.

Following the defeat of Bragg at Missionary Ridge and his own failure to take Knoxville, General Longstreet decided to move up the roads further into east Tennessee. He could not return to Bragg since Grant had followed Bragg into Georgia and was now resting between the two Confederate Armies, thus, Longstreet's best move was to re-open communications with Virginia through Bristol. To this end his command was put on the road for Rogersville on December 3rd.

General Martin was ordered to move his cavalry to the area of Morristown, Chucky Bend and Bulls Gap, unite with Ransom's Division at the latter place and clear the area of marauding Federal cavalry. On December 11th camp was made at Bulls Gap after a hard march up from Knoxville in six days of icy streams and tall hills. A two day lull here was given over to shoeing horses and collecting forage. The regimental reports for this period indicate that clothing was still sadly lacking in the Arkansas Regiment, but the men were fairly well fed. This was Union country as most of the inhabitants of east Tennessee were thoroughly loyal to the North. This made foraging easy since little sympathy was displayed by the gray horsemen for edible property in the area. On the 13th Brownlow's Brigade of east Tennessee Federals, (held in contempt by the Confederates), raided the outpost line of the Third Arkansas capturing Private James White before they were driven off.

On December 14th both cavalry commands were ordered to Russellville and from this place to Beans Station and Rutledge to drive off the Kentucky Cavalry foraging the countryside on the fringes of Longstreet's area. The command was split. Martin with Harrison's Brigade leading was to move up the Russellville-Beans Station Road while Giltner's Brigade of Ransom's Division was to move cross-country coming into the Beans Station-Rogersville Road and attack the Federals in rear. At noon the Texans and Arkansans drove in the Federals with a rush and dismounted in front of their trenchworks. Wiggins was soon blasting away at them with case shot and shell. Two hours passed while the expected Giltner never showed up. There were some hot words and hotter replies later when Martin accused Giltner of dawdling. Giltner claims he got lost in the maize of creek bottoms and canyons, (highly possible when one views this country). In any case, Martin drew off and closed the action.

On the 15th of December, Martin's scouts brought in word that a new force and a new enemy were approaching on the Rutledge Road in the person of a hard riding, hard fighting Federal General named Edward M. McCook. McCook had a formidable force, all well-trained and well-disciplined. Martin lost no time in closing with him. McCook's advanced elements were five miles east of Rutledge when the Texans and Arkansans struck. The fierceness of their attack on the bitter cold morning of December 16th carried with it surprise and success. The Pennsylvanians recoiled under the charge and broke up when the wild westerners closed with them with their six-shooters blazing. When Russell's Brigade entered the fray, the Federals broke. Once again the horse race was on. Blue horsemen dropped in steady rhythm scattering in huddled death along the streets. On into the countryside they went, not halting until McCook's main body was struck at Powder Springs. This time the Arkansans left behind some of their own. Privates Garland, Garner, Chamblis, Chambers, Edwards and Chandler were shot from their saddles and left in the hands of the enemy.

By December 19th, the enemy had been cleared from the Richland Creek Valley but he was gathering on the main road below New Market. Perceiving the danger to the Army's rear, Martin doubled back across the Holston and went into camp at Mossy Creek Station on the railroad. The Third Arkansas was assigned picket duty on the road to Dandridge where for four days the monotony was unbroken. On Christmas Eve the easy living ended.

McCook meant to break through. His entire command was launched at the same hour. Coming by every bridle path and track, they poured into the Dandridge Road and piled into Russell's Brigade in front while taking Armstrong's Division in flank. Being too far south to catch the brunt of the action, Harrison's Brigade missed the first day's battle. Russell's Alabamians fought like men possessed to hold the roadway long enough for his and Armstrong's troopers to withdraw behind Mossy Creek. When the fight was in full swing, Martin brought up Crew's Brigade, routed them around the Federal left and ordered them to charge the rear of the Federal lines. This they did in gallant style. Riding full tilt into the artillery guard, they killed or captured every man and hooking the prolong ropes to the gun trails attemped to drag them off the field. The prize was not to be. The Michiganders rode into the fray and a bloody hand-to-hand fight surged across the fileds. Maior Baie of the Sixth Georiga fell among the guns after receiving multiple wounds from sabres and pistols.

Morgan and Dibrell were now thrown into the fray and a series of charges and counter-charges surged over the fields. Wiggins' Battery hammered away at every opening with case and canister, his booming shots blending with the steady crash of carbines and pistols. One heavy charge by Campbell's Federals was beaten off by rifle butts used as clubs by Russell's dismounted men who sledged the blue coats out of their saddles. By nightfall Martin was in command of the field. The Federals had been driven from position to position finally giving up the fight, but they did not break and run. The Rebels had met their match. In the hilt-to-hilt fighting the Yankees had given as well as they had taken. Christmas Day was spent gathering the wounded and burying the dead, and there were plenty of both.

At daylight on the 27th, Martin had his full force up and mounted and another unsuccessful effort was made to dislodge the Federals. By now the fighting was concentrating between the railroad on the left and a range of hills just short of the Holston River on the right. Here there were rolling fields broken by rail and stone fences interspersed with farmhouses and barns with wooded hills on both flanks. By dawn on the 29th Martin was once again ready to assault the waiting Federals.

He formed his command with Russell's and Crew's Brigades on the left and Harrison's and Dibrell's Brigades on the right and the Horse Artillery in the center. As soon as daylight allowed, the assault was launched. This time the battle was to be carried on foot with the horses close at hand in case of repulse. By 9 a. m. the contest was fairly joined. The Federal pickets were driven back on the main body in complete confusion. Wiggins wheeled his guns forward by hand blasting away with percussion shell at every halt. His rapid shifting of position and deadly accurate fire caused one experienced Yankee Artillerist to comment that the Rebels must have been well supplied with batteries since they seemed to open from many positions at once. Again he said that on one occasion the Rebels wheeled up a four-gun battery at point-blank range and rained shells among them with pin-point accuracy.

By noon the Federals had been driven back to the banks of the creek where the brigades of Harrison, Dibrell and Crews were ordered to charge and close with them. With a wild yell they broke across the rocky fields and charged into the fray. The Arkansans and Texans striking the extreme right of the Federal position went in with rifle butts and pistols. At close quarters the fighting was murderous until the Kentucky Brigade rode into them slashing and hacking with their sabres. They gave way. Backing slowly toward the woods in the rear, they loaded and fired as fast as nervous hands could perform the motions.

At this point the brave Federals moved forward in mass, bayonets fixed in a magnificent charge. Only a stern and bloody defense by the Georgians saved the field.

Later in the afternoon, the remounted Federals made three separate efforts to break the Confederate line in mounted charges. Each time the Arkansans and Texans beat them off. Throughout the entire fracas the artillery continued to roar. Lilly's Battery of Federal Artillery was nearly destroyed in the action. The battery commander said that they had fired a hundred rounds of canister into the Rebel lines and still had had their gunners picked off by the gray clad marksmen. At 3 p. m. the One Hundred and Eighth Ohio Infantry appeared on the field and charged Wiggin's Battery. They suffered crippling losses from the double-shotted canister poured into them by Wiggins' brave Arkansans who stood manfully to their guns.

The field was still a stalemate when at 4 p. m. cheering was heard from the Federal lines and the unnerving sight of a miles long column of blue horsemen was seen coming on at a gallop up the Dandridge Road. This was Colonel O. H. LaGrange's crack Brigade of cavalry riding to the sound of the guns. A stampede was made by the Rebels for the held horses in the rear, a foot race that was won by a hair's breadth. As they formed to leave the field, LaGrange's leading regiments charged into them. Morgan's Division counter-charged and drove them off and the Rebels left the field unmolested. In his report of the battle Martin said, "The Third Arkansas, that gallant little regiment, left the field without a cartridge in the command."

The Battle of Mossy Creek had been a bloody affair. Every regiment in the command had suffered heavily in the close fighting. In some regiments, especially the Georgia formations, every officer was killed or wounded. The Third Arkansas came off light in one of the freak battle results that sometimes happen in combat. One officer and five men were down; Lieutenant R. M. Wiley and Privates Sutton, Sammons, Griffith, Hobson and Hale were wounded and left on the field too badly hurt to bring off. The entire family of the Regimental Commander was rapidly being killed off. The regiment was in bad shape as was most of the command. They were ragged, barefoot and had no blankets, and the weather was bitter cold. Not a man in the command had been paid in six months and none was in the offing. The Confederacy was slowly dying on the vine.

The early weeks of January were given over to constant scouting and patroling over the frozen roads from Chucky Bend to Newport. On January 28th a probing column of Federals attempted to penetrate the screen below Dandridge and the command was called to saddle. This was Campbell's Brigade of McCook's Division. Once again Dibrell and Harrison carried the fight. It was brief and bloody. The Federals were driven for miles down the road leading to Strawberry Plains. In the hot race that followed the rout of the Yankees, Privates Henry DeSpain, W. B. Walter and Abraham Plunkett were badly wounded. This was the last of the heavy action for the winter.

In early February, the Rebels had a grand opportunity to wreak vengeance on Brownlow's Yankee Tennesseeans. While patroling north of Newport, Brownlow encountered two companies of Alabamians of Morgan's Command and routed them. The fleeing Rebels led the hot pursuit Federals right into Harrison's Brigade returning from a scout. Without hesitation the Arkansans and Texans piled in. The shocked Federals had no time to collect their wits before the Rebels were among them. They simply broke and scattered in every direction. When the fired up Confederates were through with the roundup, Brownlow was no longer a threat in eastern Tennessee.

During the month of February the sole enemy was hunger. The roads were impassable and the weather was murderous in the Tennessee Mountains. Wagons could not be employed on the roads, so the foragers had to operate strictly on horseback over the narrow trails, bringing in supplies tied to the saddles. While engaged in this business, they often encountered some of the numerous bushwhackers in the rugged hills. Private James Drain was killed by one of these skulkers on February 11th. On February 22nd Privates Foulkes and Whitney were captured by one of many marauding bands of murderers prowling in the hills and were never heard of again.

In early April, Longstreet's Infantry left the hills of Tennessee and moved on to Virginia to rejoin Lee for the Spring campaign. This movement removed any reason for the cavalry to remain in the area. It was with heartfelt gratitude that orders were received for the gray horsemen to move into North Georgia and rejoin General Wheeler and the main army now under General Joseph E. Johnston. A slow and pleasant march was made up the French Broad River Valley and down into western

North Carolina. Through Marshal, Ashville and Hendersonville and on into western South Carolina they rode. At Pickens they turned westward and on April 25th rode into the cavalry camps of Johnston's Army at Dalton.

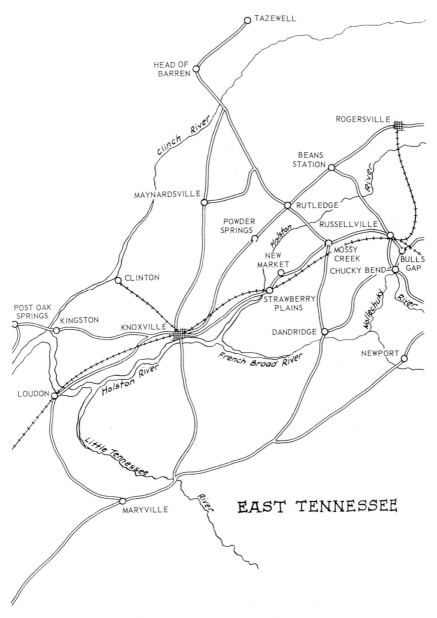

Chapter X

ATLANTA

General Joseph Johnston was back in command. The camps were clean, spirits were high, morale was good and things were generally humming. The change from Bragg to Johnston was near miraculous and was readily apparent to any visitor to the camps. It was also obvious that campaigning was in the offing. Beyond Tunnel Hill and Rocky Face Ridge the Federals were massing. General William T. Sherman was in command over there and he was no idler.

Grant had been called to Washington and given command of all the Armies of the Union, and he had placed Sherman in command of the massive armies facing Johnston. Lincoln had at last found the perfect combination in Grant and Sherman, a discovery that was to win a war. Grant's plan was simple and blunt—move out, gain contact, maintain that contact and fight. He would personally lead the army against Lee in Virginia and Sherman was to assail Johnston and fight him to a conclusion. Atlanta, Georgia was to be the object point of his march and Johnston's Army the target. May 3rd, 1864 was to be their D-Day.

In the Confederate camps, Johnston was getting ready. He was calling in his scattered forces and reorganizing them into fighting commands under fighting leaders. His infantry corps commanders were Generals William J. Hardee, Leonidas Polk and John B. Hood.

The cavalry was assigned to General Joseph Wheeler and he lost no time reorganizing this arm into a first class fighting force. The amalgamation of the division from east Tennessee with the horsemen already with the main army made a sizeable force.

Brig. General W. Y. C. Humes

Colonel Thomas Harrison

Colonel George Dibrell

Colonel William W. Allen

Wheeler organized the cavalry into three divisions under Generals William T. Martin, John H. Kelly and William Y. C. Humes.

Martin's Division consisted of the Brigades of Brigadier Generals John T. Morgan and Alfred Iverson. Kelly's Division had Brigadier General W. W. Allen's Brigade and Colonel George Dibrell's Brigade. Humes' Division was made up of the Brigades commanded by Colonels J. T. Wheeler, Thomas Harrison, J. Warren Grigsby and M. W. Hannon.

Harrison's Brigade remained the same—Third Arkansas, Eighth Texas, Eleventh Texas and Fourth Tennessee. This time they were associated with the gallant fighters from Kentucky in Grigsby's famous Brigade and the hard riding Tennesseeans of Wheeler's Brigade. In addition, General Humes was a first class fighting man and a fine commander. It made a happy outfit. By May 1st, the Rebel troopers were ready for the field.

When the campaign opened, the gray cavalrymen were picketing the entire front of the army. Their lines extended from Ships Gap on the left, far along the line of hills to the Connesauga River on the right. Harrison's Brigade held the center of the line astride the Dalton-Chattanooga Road. On May 5, 1864 the Federals launched the campaign that was to win the war. As Grant was crossing the Rapidan in Virginia, Sherman was moving against Rocky Face Ridge north of Dalton. Contact was gained that same day and was never broken until the issue was decided.

May 5th and 6th were given over to feeble attempts by the Confederate horsemen to obstruct the roads between the lines. This work availed them nothing when Sherman's mighty army of ninety-eight thousand men and two hundred fifty-four guns struck. Wheeler's men were first to feel them. In front of Rocky Face at Tunnel Hill, Harrison and Dibrell's Brigades skirmished with them throughout the day and far into the night. On the 7th Wheeler massed his horse artillery along the railroad and hammered away at them causing considerable delay and confusion. Late in the day General O. O. Howard moved his infantry forward in force and drove the Rebel Cavalry from the field. They retreated through the village and moved behind the main infantry lines along Rocky Face and regained their horses.

Grigsby's Brigade was dispatched to Dug Gap just before daylight on the 8th and the rest of the command was moved to

the Cleveland Road to meet a heavy force advancing from that
direction. Beginning on this date and for many months to come,
the steady rumble of heavy battle maintained an incessant echo.
While Grigsby's men fought a vicious delaying battle at Dug Gap
their comrades in arms also entered the fray. McCook's Division
of cavalry spearheading an infantry advance were moving forward
on the Cleveland Road when the "War Child" hit him. Allen's
and Dibrell's Brigades were dismounted and sent forward on foot
while Harrison's Texans and Arkansans followed slowly in
mounted column. As soon as contact was made Wheeler ordered
the charge. With a wild yell the dismounted men charged across
the fields driving the Federal pickets precipitately back on the
main force. Before the Yankees could regroup, the fast running
Rebels were pouring a steady hail of carbine slugs among them.
The vigilant Wheeler coming on at the head of the Texas Brigade waited until the Federals showed signs of wavering under
the fierce attack of Dibrell and Allen, then in perfect timing
sounded the commands, "Forward at a gallop—HO-O!." "Draw
pistols—CHARGE!"

The Eighth Texas and First Confederate, vying for space on
the narrow road, charged full speed into the wavering Yankees
spilling men and horses into the fields. The Federals broke.
Just as they gave way, the Eleventh Texas and Third Arkansas
struck them in both flanks and the horse race was on. At full
speed the race was over ditches, hedges and fences for five miles
across the countryside. The Rebels made capitol pistol practice,
emptying saddles in wholesale lots. The sabre was freely used
when both pistols were empty. The race didn't end until the
panicked bluecoats rode at racing speed into the waiting arms of
their own infantry. When the dust had settled a hundred and
twenty-five prisoners were being herded along the road and
another hundred and ten Federals would fight no more. Private
John Haynie of the Eighth Texas had the prize of the chase.
He rode up to General Harrison with Colonel LaGrange of the
Indiana Brigade riding in front of him in the saddle. Harrison
greeted his old opponent from east Tennessee warmly and was
told that LaGrange had been promised his Brigadier General's
star if his advance was successful. Harrison told him sympathetic-
ally, "It's the fortunes of war, my friend," and sent him off to
the prison pens.

On the 11th Wheeler's scouts reported that General George
Stoneman, a throw-off from Grant's Army in Virginia, was
advancing in heavy force toward Varnell's Station and if unin-

General Joseph E. Johnston   Lt. General John B. Hood

Maj. General W. T. Sherman U.S.A.   Maj General George Stoneman U.S.A.

hibited would soon be in the Confederate rear. Within an hour the graybacks were hammering up the road. Halfway to Varnells, Kelly's Division was picked up and added to the column. Here Wheeler split the command. Kelly was sent off to the right to come in on Stoneman's flank while he, with Humes' Division, continued straight ahead up the railroad. Still keeping with the philosophy that audacity and will must triumph over numbers, Wheeler piled in. The wild Kentuckians struck the head of Stoneman's column full in front in a murderous charge while the Texans and Arkansans careened along their flanks firing point blank into them with their six shooters.

The impetuosity of Wheeler's attack was truly a blessing in this fight. Stoneman's massive force was spread out over nearly five miles of road outnumbering the Rebels at least two to one. In addition, a commissary supply train two miles long was moving at the rear of the mounted force. The Federals never got around to fighting. They broke for the main army in wild flight with Allen's men flailing them out of the saddles. The supply train guards panicked and burned the entire train before Harrison's troops could save them. Tons of supplies went up in flames along with four hundred wagons. One hundred and fifty Federals were killed or captured in the rat race for Rocky Face Ridge.

After dark Wheeler was informed that Sherman was swinging wide around Johnston's left and was rapidly approaching Resaca. The army was to abandon the present line and fall back to prevent Sherman from getting in their rear. The cavalry was to occupy the forward trenches allowing the infantry to fall back in the night to Resaca. With the held horses in the rear, the Rebel cavalrymen fought a tough delaying action all day on the 13th. Fighting, withdrawing and fighting until 3 p. m. they were relieved by an infantry brigade at Tilton. Here the two forces formed an L-shaped line and fought it out until 9 p. m. when the Federal attacks died off.

The day of the 14th was repetitious of the 13th, the command being stuck with trench fighting until 3 p. m. when Wheeler was ordered to return to the right flank of the army beyond the Connesauga River. On this date the bloody battle of Resaca was fought between the two contending giants and ended with Sherman once again sideling around to the right turning Johnston out of his works.

After daylight on the 15th of May, Sherman's Army was pouring across the Oostanaula far below Resaca and headed for

Calhoun on the Western and Atlantic Railroad. Stoneman's Cavalry, spearheading the Federal advance, slipped into the retreating Confederate lines and stumbled into the hospitals of Hardee's Corps. Just as he was beginning his work of destruction of this vital area, Wheeler's hard riding Rebels sailed into them. Once again Humes' Division was in front and Harrison's Brigade had the point. One charge did the trick again. The Federals were driven four miles back to their infantry losing forty prisoners and two regimenal colors.

From May 15th through the 23rd the cavalry fought as infantry. Day after day in the blistering heat they fought and withdrew. Each time the main army made a stand, Sherman turned their flank until the retreat had carried them below the Etowah. Johnston was exacting a fearful price for every yard of ground given up and was still hoping for an opportunity to strike Sherman a crippling blow. The weary Confederate infantryman fought and died over the countryside in one long, continuous battle, a situation planned by Sherman knowing that attrition was the answer to defeating this battle wise army of veteran soldiers.

At midnight on the 23rd Wheeler was ordered to strike the enemy rear in the neighborhood of Cassville, determine his position and destroy any supplies found in the area. Before daylight the command was on the road. The First Georgia was sent on to Cass Station to decoy the enemy in that direction while Wheeler led Humes' and Kelly's Divisions around the Federal right and struck for Cassville. Reaching the outskirts of the town, Wheeler formed Humes' Division in rear of the town to protect his attacking force if defeated and led Kelly's Division straight in. In a thunderous charge, Kelly scattered the Federals in the town and discovered an immense supply train on the road. Eighty wagons were captured and two hundred burned before the Federals could regroup.

Bringing off the wagons was not as easy as their capture. Kelly was so weakened by details of men to drive the teams and destroy the railroad, he could not defend himself. Halfway between Cass Station and Cassville, Stoneman tore into the rearguard and the battle was on. Wheeler was determined to save the precious wagons and put up a terrific fight. The action was hanging in the balance when the faithful Humes appeared riding to the sound of the guns. Coming up on the fight Humes formed Harrison's and Wheeler's Brigades in line and Grigsby's Brigade in column and charged in. There followed a unique battle action. The ground was chewed up so often and so thoroughly by the heavy military traffic that the dust was eight inches deep and as fine as talcum powder. When collision was made at full charge the dust boiled up so thick that a horse couldn't be distinguished at arms length. The Confederates got off one volley from their pistols then both sides mingled in the dust cloud stumbling and colliding on horseback with no way of knowing who was rubbing elbows and knees—friend or foe. The Federals drew off from the action, and Wheeler brought out his wagons. That night the dust was settled. One of the worst thunderstorms in the memory of the local inhabitants struck. The rain came down in rivers and the lightning was fearful. Camp was made in sight of the Federals without molestation since nothing could move in the storm. By 9 a. m. men and wagons were safe behind the army below the Etowah.

At this point in the history of the Third Arkansas Cavalry the detailed records of the regiment end. Though their battle records exist, the Morning Reports and Muster Rolls were burned in North Carolina in April of 1865 and are lost to history.

Days of skirmishing both afoot and on horseback continued while the main army fought it out. The terrible battles at New Hope Church, Dallas, Kennesaw Mountain and Smyrna were fought, always ending with the persistent Sherman flanking the slowly shrinking Rebel Army. At Kennesaw, Sherman threw his army against Johnston's trenches in a stupid attack and saw them slaughtered at a fearful rate. Nothing daunted, and daily resupplied with men and supplies, Sherman hammered on and on July 9th saw Johnston retreat into the Atlanta defenses. Here the Confederacy suffered a heavy blow. President Jefferson Davis relieved General Joseph E. Johnston and appointed in his stead, General John Bell Hood. Hood was a fighter but was far from being a Johnston. The army leadership made no effort to hide their chagrin and displeasure at the change. While the Rebels cursed the change, Sherman rejoiced. The Federal Commander had profound respect for Johnston, but was confident he could whip Hood in short order.

On July 20th Hood struck. He threw in half his army at Peach Tree Creek in front of Atlanta and was soundly defeated and driven back into the trenchworks. Sherman closed forward and the siege of Atlanta was on.

On this same date, Wheeler was sent to the southeast face

Brig. General L. S. Ross

Brig. General S. W. Ferguson

Brig. General John S. Williams

Brig. General Alfred Iverson

of the Atlanta works to oppose the advance of McPherson's Army Corps in that sector. Dismounting his entire command, they entered the fight. Throughout the long hot July day, the Rebels fought a hard delaying battle and at darkness were barely holding their own. At daylight they were relieved by the grizzled veterans of Patrick Cleburne. One wonders at the exchange of conversation when the Third Arkansas Cavalry was relieved by the famous Arkansas Brigade of Cleburne's Division. These tough veterans had suffered many bloody combats on the long retreat and were rated the top unit in the army.

On withdrawing from the front, Wheeler had time to look at his new troops. General W. H. Jackson had arrived from Mississippi with his fine division of Frank C. Armstrong's Brigade, General L. S. Ross' famous Texas Brigade and General S. W. Ferguson's Brigade. Brigadier General John S. Williams was now in command of Grigsby's famous Kentucky Brigade. General Philip D. Roddy's Brigade of Rangers was also on the scene from north Mississippi but were in bad shape from hard campaigning.

On the night of the 21st of July Wheeler was ordered to move to attack Decatur in coordination with a massive effort by Hardee's Corps to flank and destroy the Federal left below the Georgia Railroad. This effort was made with a portion of the cavalry since several brigades were scattered about the country on picket duty watching the movements of the Federal mounted force. Harrison's Brigade was on this duty patroling the roads from East Point toward Palmetto and therefore missed the action at Decatur.

Wheeler's action was to no avail. The bloody Battle of Atlanta was fought on the 22nd in which once again the Confederates had too little to do too big a job. The battle was carried with fierce zeal but the strength was not there. It ended in stalemate with both sides in their same positions and the siege of Atlanta became a fixed fact.

Sherman now decided to break the railroads leading into Atlanta in order to put the strangle on Hood's Army occupying the impregnable trenches. He called in his cavalry commanders and issued the orders. Stoneman was given General Garrard's Division in addition to his own and ordered to leave the left of the army near Decatur, swing wide to Covington, destroy the Georgia Railroad at this point, move on to Macon and break up the Macon and Western Railroad. He was to be joined before Macon by General E. M. McCook's Division who would leave the right of the army, crossing the river at Riverton, smash the Atlanta and West Point Railroad at Palmetto, ride on to Lovejoy's Station on the Macon and Western, meet Stoneman at this point and jointly wreck the railroad south to Macon. At this point Stoneman requested authority to unite with McCook at or near Lovejoy's, then move far south to Andersonville and release the Federal prisoners at the camp and bring them back into the lines. Sherman reluctantly approved this last request and wished them luck. This was the undoing of an otherwise brilliantly planned maneuver.

At noon on July 27th, while relieving Hardee's Infantry Corps in the trenches southeast of Atlanta, Wheeler learned that Garrard's horsemen had crossed the railroad and were striking for Flat Rock south of the city. Wheeler promptly relieved Allen's Brigade from the trenches and started them for Flat Rock. By nightfall he had Dibrell's Brigade on the road and was hammering southward. The balance of the command was ordered to move southward as soon as they were clear of the trenches. It was 9 p. m. when Wheeler approached Flat Run Shoals and heard the steady splatter of rifle fire. Wheeler held on through the night and at daylight routed Dibrell's Brigade around Garrard's left-rear and then attacked him in front with Allen's men. This action broke the Yankee hold on the Flat Rock Road and sent them reeling back toward Decatur.

General Garrard had been abandoned and he didn't know it. Stoneman had no intention of going to Flat Rock. He was swinging wide around to the east and striking for Covington. He intended to move direct to Macon and thence on to Andersonville. George Stoneman was glory hunting.

By darkness on the 28th, Wheeler was aware that Stoneman was beyond his right and moving south. He instantly devined the Federal intention. He called in General Alfred Iverson and gave him Allen's Brigade and the Kentucky Brigade temporarily under Colonel W. C. P. Breckenridge and sent him in pursuit of Stoneman. At this time, too, Wheeler was informed that a heavy force of Federal cavalry under McCook was across the Chattahoochee at Riverton and striking for the railroad at Palmetto. He was being assailed on both flanks at once. Leaving Stoneman to Iverson, Wheeler struck out cross-country toward Rough and Ready. With him he took Colonel Wheeler's old brigade now under Colonel H. M. Ashby and General Humes who was traveling with him. Cutting southward Wheeler rode into Jonesboro,

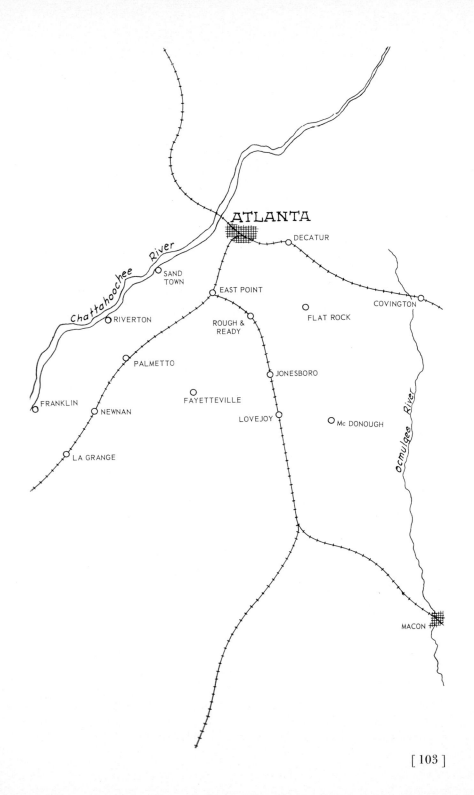

ATLANTA

DECATUR

Chattahoochee River

SAND
TOWN

EAST POINT

COVINGTON

RIVERTON

FLAT ROCK

ROUGH &
READY

PALMETTO

JONESBORO

Ocmulgee River

FRANKLIN

FAYETTEVILLE

NEWNAN

LOVEJOY

Mc DONOUGH

LA GRANGE

MACON

the town he knew to be the objective point of McCook's march, at 4 p. m.

While the commanding general was formulating his plans, the Third Arkansas was fighting. Harrison's alert scouts had reported McCook's presence as soon as he was over the river. He immediately made contact and skirmishing began. Falling slowly back toward Palmetto he was joined by the Texas Brigade under General Ross at this point. Before the two small Confederate commands could gain effective position to fight, McCook's determined Federals had crossed the railroad and moved on to Fayetteville. Here the wagon burning took a new turn. The hard riding Yankees rode right into General Jackson's entire cavalry supply train. In a matter of a few hours some four hundred wagons were burned and eight hundred mules were killed.

At this point Harrison and Ross piled in, fighting McCook to a standstill. Here, too, McCook's scouts reported that the supposed rendezvous with Stoneman and Garrard was a fiction. They had been all the way to Lovejoy's Station and beyond, and not a Yankee was in sight. There were plenty of Rebels, however. Wheeler now rode on the scene with Ashby's Brigade and put the pressure on the Federals. McCook, now with the smell of disaster in the air, decided to retreat for his unprotected river crossings.

McCook was not aware of it but Garrard had been routed at Flat Creek and driven back behind the Federal Army. His victors were now galloping to the fray with McCook. Stoneman had fared worse. Iverson had ridden furiously over the countryside coming up with Stoneman below Covington and, in a series of brilliant actions, pulverized the Federal column capturing Stoneman and most of his command. Only a handful of demoralized fugitives survived to reach safety at Atlanta.

In McCook's column, Armstrong had charged into his rear files nearly wrecking Croxton's crack Brigade and stampeding the pack mules over the landscape.

Wheeler now closed in. Ross' Texans were sent on a wild ride to cut off McCook's escape route near Newnan while Harrison and Ashby continued to press his rear. Anderson had been severely wounded during the day and Colonel Edward Bird was in command of his brigade. Bird was sent to press the left flank of the Federals on the La Grange-Newnan Road. When McCook's now near-panicked command reached Newnan, he found the town occupied by Roddy's fierce command. He detoured southward to the La Grange Road and rode right into Ashby's Brigade supported by Bird. McCook was driven to ground.

Ross' Texans and part of Harrison's Brigade were dismounted and sent in. The Texans made a wild, fierce attack on the cornered Federals. They could smell the victory and nothing would stop them. The fighting was close and deadly in the dense woods fronting on the road. McCook was rapidly losing his command when he ordered every regimental commander to fight his way out the best way possible. In the ensuing melee the Eighth Iowa broke into the held horses of the Texas Brigade and captured General Ross and a large body of his men. Ross was promptly rescued by Ashby's Brigade and the Iowans were scattered to the wind.

When the Federals broke, Wheeler ordered Colonel McKenzie to take his own regiment and the Third Arkansas and cut McCook off from the Chattahoochee Fords near Franklin. They had travelled some six miles at a gallop when the retreating enemy hove into view. McKenzie ordered Colonel Hobson to move to the right across a series of cornfields and assail the Federals in front while he rode on ahead to come in on the Yankee rear. As soon as the regiment was clear of the road, Hobson ordered the regiment to "ON RIGHT—FORWARD INTO LINE!". Still going at a trot he waited until the last fours rode into line, then standing in the stirrups, he yelled, "FORWARD AT A GALLOP—CHARGE!"

The standing corn was laid flat on the ground by the onrushing horsemen. Riding flat out, screaming like banshees, the Arkansans smashed into the disordered Federals. Horses and riders were knocked over like bowling pins in the battering ram charge. Six shooters in the hands of experts blazed away, slashing sabres glittered in the sunlight. McKenzie's men charged into the fray shooting and cutting. It was short and vicious. When the dust settled eighty-five dead Federals were scattered over the fields and another three hundred and fifty were being herded together as prisoners. The remnant of McCook's command scattered to the woods and individually made their way over the river to safety behind the main army at Atlanta.

In this affray the Third Arkansas lost one Lieutenant killed and several men and officers wounded. It had been a signal victory indeed. In three days the hard riding Rebels had nearly destroyed a total cavalry force of 9,000 men. Stoneman and most of his command were captured, Garrard was driven off, beaten and demoralized, and McCook's column had been broken up and routed. Three thousand Federals had been captured and another two thousand killed or scattered. In addition, vast quantities of materiel and hundreds of horses fell into Wheeler's hands. This masterful piece of mounted deployment and action made of little Joseph Wheeler a great man in the eyes of the Confederate people and their government, and served to consolidate his own men behind him for the first time. The "War Child's Children" had performed exceedingly well.

Chapter XI

On August 8th General Hood sent for General Wheeler where he received orders for a new and hazardous enterprise. Hood felt that Sherman's Army was entirely dependent on the railroads leading south from Nashville and if these railroads could be broken up, Sherman just might give up the siege of Atlanta and retreat northward. In reality it was a desperation move since it was already evident that Sherman's railroad crews could repair a road almost as fast as the Rebel raiders could tear it up. Nevertheless, Wheeler was ordered to take all the cavalry except Jackson's Division, move northward breaking up the railroad between Cassville and Dalton then slide northeastward into east Tennessee. Here he was to cross this mighty river into central Tennessee and smash up things around Nashville. The operational details were left entirely to Wheeler.

Two days after receiving his orders, Wheeler was ready. He set his command at three divisions under Generals Martin, Humes and Kelly. Martin was to have the brigades of Allen, Iverson and the newly assigned brigade of Texans under Felix Robertson. Humes with Ashby's, Harrison's and Hannon's Brigades and Kelly's command consisted of the brigades of Anderson, Dibrell and Williams. On August 10th, 1864 the second Tennessee raid was under way.

Crossing the Chattahoochee at Campbelltown, the command struck the railroad at Marietta. By nightfall ten miles of railroad were devastated and the horsemen moved on to Cassville and Calhoun. Here on the 12th, Hannon's Brigade captured a herd of beef cattle numbering 1,700 animals and dozens of wagons. Knowing the starving condition of the army, Wheeler ordered Hannon to move his valuable prize eastward to Ellijay in north central Georgia, then make his way back to Atlanta by any route he could manage. Hannon returned to Atlanta with but trifling loss of his stock, an accomplishment of some magnitude when one considers the great distance and the fact that every mile was through enemy held territory.

On August 14th, Humes' Division appeared before Dalton, a major supply point on Sherman's line. The Rebel demand for surrender was refused so the place was carried in a vicious charge by the division supported by Allen's Brigade. The garrison was routed in panic by the onrushing horsemen, the survivors retreating into a strong blockhouse north of the town. Dalton was a big haul. Hundreds of tons of food and ammunition were found along with some three hundred wagons and six hundred horses and mules. Two hundred prisoners were paroled and twelve miles of track were ripped up and burned. Wheeler demonstrated here his new-found ability to maintain discipline in his command. He had ordered General Martin to move northward ripping up the track while Wheeler moved south to meet him. This Martin failed to do. He had gone into camp scarce ten miles away and Wheeler had no idea where he was. Martin was promptly relieved of command, placed under arrest and sent back to the army at Atlanta. General Iverson was given his division for the raid.

While moving out of Dalton at daylight, Humes' Division, acting as rearguard, was assailed by a Federal Cavalry Brigade under General Steedman. The fight was hardly in progress before Humes ordered Ashby and Harrison to charge them full in front. The Federals broke as soon as they were struck. The Arkansans and Texans drove them four miles killing several men including one colonel and wounding General Steedman. They were not molested again below the Tennessee.

On the 15th, Williams' Brigade destroyed the railroad from Tunnel Hill to Graysville burning many bridges and obstructing tunnels. At this place, Wheeler stayed on the road until the 21st thoroughly demolishing the roadbed, breaking water towers and burning wood. On the 22nd the command was ordered to the Hiawassee River area near Columbus in Tennessee. The horses were in bad shape and rapidly foundering for lack of grain. The only forage available in north Georgia was new corn so soft it could be mashed with the fingers and the animals were dying on their feet on this poor food. On the Hiawassee there was plenty of last year's corn and fodder and here the command was rapidly improved, both men and animals.

The "War Child" didn't linger to rebuild his command. He simply passed through the country, building up his horses as he traveled. During the 24th and 25th his wreckers struck the railroad from Cleveland to Charleston and then Charleston to Loudon. Nearly fifty miles of trackage were destroyed and dozens of bridges were burned. At Stewart's Landing on the Holston, three hundred badly needed horses were captured and two hundred prisoners paroled.

Wheeler intended to cross the Tennessee at Cotton Port and follow his old route into central Tennessee, but the river was up ten feet and far past fording. Now pressed for time the Rebel Raiders struck eastward riding hard for the upper Holston and Clinch Rivers. Before Knoxville, a rag-tag force of east Tennessee Federals attacked the column and were scattered to the hills by Kelly's Division who killed or captured two hundred of them.

On August 27th, the hard pressing troopers passed through Rutledge having crossed the French Broad and Holston Rivers by the upper fords and were now moving westward toward Kingston. Here Wheeler lost control of a large portion of his command. General Williams talked Wheeler into giving him his own and Dibrell's Brigades and half the artillery for the purpose of striking the railroad and bridge at Strawberry Plains, destroy this vital place and then rejoin the command. The Commanding General reluctantly approved the request and never saw these units again for months. Williams failed to destroy the bridge or the railroad; followed Wheeler into central Tennessee; failed to rejoin and later retreated out of the state.

Through Post Oak Springs and Pikeville the command moved on and in early September appeared before McMinnville. This depot was again destroyed along with an entire train of cars and the raiders moved on through Woodbury to Murfreesboro. At this place the command was broken up into brigade level and set upon the railroad between Murfreesboro and Chattanooga. The horsemen worked like Trojans for days. The line was completely smashed for seventy-five miles above and below Murfreesboro.

By now the hornet's nest was stirred up. The Official Records contain dozens of dispatches, letters and telegrams between various Federal Commands indicating near panic at Wheeler's appearance in central Tennessee. Williams and Dibrell had belatedly followed the main Rebel force adding to the Federal confusion. These bits of correspondence are ludicrous today when viewed in retrospect. Williams is shown as having a formidable force and striking in every direction. Dibrell is here—there—and everywhere, sometimes in four or five places at once. Actually, both Dibrell and Williams were desperately trying to reach Wheeler but were being pressed from every direction by Federal Cavalry. Finally on September 6th, Dibrell's small Brigade was cornered at Readyville by Brigadier General John T. Croxton's large mounted force and routed. Dibrell was encumbered by nearly two hundred new recruits who were without arms or horses and in attempting to defend these helpless men he lost his mobility. In the ensuing fight Dibrell was driven nearly back to Pikeville. He later made his way back over the mountains into east Tennessee.

Williams was driven from place to place all over the southern area of middle Tennessee. His absence did help Wheeler in one respect—he drew off part of the pursuit. In addition to Dibrell and Williams, Brigadier General Felix Robertson's Brigade was detached from the main column and was smashing up the railroads around Cowan, Decherd, Winchester and Fayetteville. Large bodies of Federal Infantry and Cavalry pursued him all over the landscape but he managed to elude them all and reached safety beyond the Tennessee at Mussel Shoals.

Meanwhile, with the main column, things were heating up. The confused Federals were slowly gaining order out of the chaos of conflicting orders. Major Generals L. H. Rousseau and Joseph B. Steedman and Brigadier Generals Croxton and Granger with large forces of cavalry and infantry were closing in on Wheeler. While breaking up the road near Antioch, Rousseau collided with Humes' Division protecting the wreckers. Humes sent in Ashby's Brigade as decoy and soon had Rousseau's lead elements pounding down the road in hot pursuit. These Federal garrison soldiers had a lot to learn. Harrison's Brigade of howling Texans and Arkansans rode down their flanks while Ashby doubled back on the head of the column. The Federals broke in wild flight for Nashville, the horse race going at full speed for three miles where the fleeing blue coats reached safety in the outer trenchworks. Three regimental colors and two hundred prisoners were captured in addition to eighty-five killed. In addition Ashby brought off thirty loaded wagons and sixty horses.

Wheeler had now spent ten days on the Nashville-Chattanooga line, putting it out of service for nearly a month and it

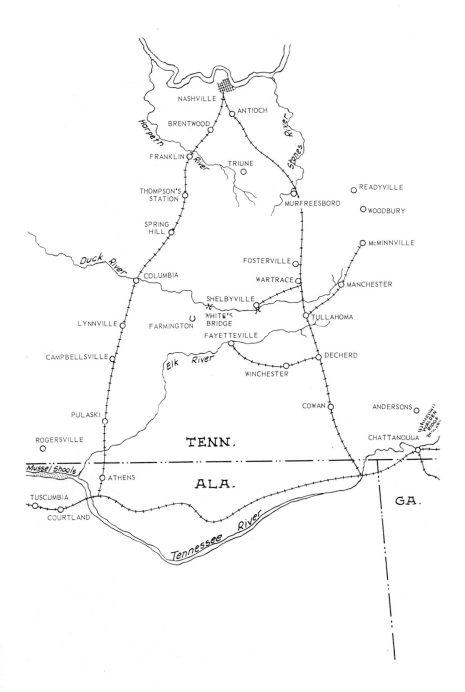

Destruction in the wake of Wheeler's Raid through middle Tennessee

Bridge at Strawberry Plains, Tennessee

was time to change locations. Sending Humes' Division toward the Hermitage northeast of Nashville as a decoy, Wheeler cut cross-country with Kelly's Division striking the Central Alabama Railroad above Brentwood. This action gave him three more days to tear up this trackage and burn bridges before Rousseau realized that he had been foxed. Once apprised of the location of the wrecking crew, Rousseau concentrated his force and struck southward. Moving between Humes and Kelly at Brentwood, and riding hard through the night, he came up with Kelly at dawn and piled in. The Confederates, sorely outnumbered and desperately weary after weeks of ripping up railroads, were no match for the well armed, well mounted Yankees.

Shelled, charged and battered for eight miles, Kelly withdrew into the town of Franklin, where in a series of desperate countercharges the Federals were stalled off. In one of these close-quarter encounters the gallant General John H. Kelly fell mortally wounded. The fighting was still surging through the streets when the road-weary troopers under Humes entered the fray.

After riding day and night through Lavergne and Nolensville, Humes had evaded the Federal pickets below Brentwood and entered Franklin from the south. Quickly throwing Harrison's and Ashby's Brigades into a column of fours, Humes charged into the fight. Croxton's Brigade was routed in panic by the fierce westerners and driven clear through the town. Rousseau promptly counterattacked, regaining the town. Wheeler now drew off southward in the direction of Littlebury in order to regroup his battered command. Once in open country the Rebels were again in their element. Sending Iverson and Allen forward as decoys, Wheeler massed Harrison's, Ashby's and Anderson's Brigades in line behind a rise in ground and waited.

It wasn't a long wait. The Federals, now with the scent of victory in their nostrils, appeared in heavy column in thunderous pursuit of the fleeing Rebels.

As soon as the chase topped the rise, the "War Child" cut the tether. The wild screech of the Rebel Yell, a roar of hooves on the sun-baked roads and the rumble of pistol fire shattered the afternoon. Horses and men were bowled over like dominoes in the breast-to-breast collision. Back up the Pike in wild flight; pursuer and pursued in flat out speed; pistols blazing, sabres swishing; back into the streets of Franklin went the noise of war.

When the recall sounded and the gray coats drew off, not every man answered the bugle. Colonel Anson W. Hobson, the physician-turned-soldier, had fought his last fight. Shot through the upper chest and bleeding profusedly, he was brought off with Lieutenant Colonel Henderson and Major Blackwell holding him in the saddle. In addition to Colonel Hobson, the Third Arkansas left several officers and men dead or wounded in the streets of Franklin.

A spring wagon was found, loaded with hay and the wounded Colonel was placed in it and started for the Tennessee at Mussel Shoals. The able bodied went back to wrecking railroads.

At Lynnville, Rousseau and Croxton again assailed the Raiders and again they were beaten off. The process was repeated at Campbellsville and Pulaski where another murderous charge by Humes' Division stalled pursuit for two days. Wheeler was being driven from the state but he was extracting a heavy cost from his assailants. At Rogersville, the veteran brigade of General Philip D. Roddy joined the battered Rebels to aid them in crossing the Tennessee. He had crossed the river at the urging of General Nathan Forrest who had rightly assumed that Wheeler's Command was near disintegration. The advent of Roddy put just enough steel back in the demoralized raiders to give them the chance to escape to safety beyond the Tennessee. In early October, the weary Confederates went into camp below Courtland after more than a month of riding, working and fighting. General Forrest, who had an opportunity to visit the camps during this period, commented that Wheeler's Command was in a "demoralized state—completely broken down." He added that "hundreds of stragglers, some with passes, some without, were scattered over the countryside."

This time there was a good reason for the broken down condition of the command. It had been a long, hard, brutal raid. Wheeler gave Forrest some fifteen hundred men who had been left behind in Tennessee and prepared to move on to join Hood in Georgia.

While in camp near Courtland, some twelve men of the Third Arkansas organized an "Owl Train" and departed for home. Wheeler sent Captain Bass and twenty men after the recalcitrants. Bass, with his mixed force of men from the Third Arkansas and Eighth Texas, pursued the deserters nearly to the Mississippi River before they were run to ground. They were returned under guard but the records do not indicate what, if any, punishment was inflicted upon them.

Wheeler's record for this raid was an imposing one. The

Railroad bridge at Pulaski, Tenn. twice destroyed by Wheeler during the war.

command had averaged twenty-five miles a day; swam or forded twenty-seven rivers; captured or killed more Federals than he himself had taken on the raid and wrecked the Federal supply system that would take a month to repair. His total loss in killed, wounded and captured numbered one hundred and fifty. The "War Child" had pulled off a signal success.

After rest and refitting in north Alabama, Wheeler was ordered to move back to the railroad around Dalton in north Georgia and once again interrupt Sherman's communications. On October 9th the elusive Rebels charged into Dalton and once again captured the garrison. The freshly rebuilt railroad was ripped up for ten miles above and below the town before Wheeler headed southward. Near Calhoun a courier arrived in the camps with orders from Hood to proceed immediately to Cedartown and rejoin the main army. On October 15th the much traveled railroad smashers entered the lines of Hood's beaten army below the Etowah.

Chapter XII

Epilogue

The advent of winter 1864 in the Confederacy brought with it the seeds of finality. Lee's once superb army was now reduced to a starving remnant at Petersburg and Richmond and were holding on with nothing but grit. Food and forage in the Confederacy had long since disappeared and the starving, freezing troops were no better off for clothing. In Hood's defeated Army at Cedartown, demoralization was rampant. Disaster at Atlanta had been compounded by overwhelming defeat at Jonesborough. Jefferson Davis himself had appeared in the camps in order to bolster the sagging morale of the men. The magnificent Creole, General P. G. T. Beauregard, had also been there in hopes that his presence would offer distraction from inevitable loss of the Confederate States.

Despite these setbacks, General John Hood was planning big things. In his confused mind the thought had jelled that if he could get beyond Sherman's lines and in his rear, rip up the railroads, march into Tennessee and recapture Nashville, Sherman would abandon Georgia and retreat into Kentucky. In addition to this dream, Hood intended to move from Nashville all the way to Richmond to join Lee in hopes of defeating Grant with the combined armies. This scheme was beyond the wildest imagination even for an army flushed with victory and completely equipped. With the beaten, demoralized, half-starved Army of Tennessee, it was a forlorn hope at best but, as history was to record, no grander effort was ever made by any army that ever marched on this earth. The names of Franklin and Nashville were yet to be recorded on the banners of the Army of Tennessee, but Valhalla's Halls were holding a special place at the head of the list for these immortals who were marching northward through Georgia.

When General Hood had formulated his plans, he sent for General Wheeler and left him the impossible task of watching and fighting Sherman. A small, war-weary force of cavalrymen numbering less than six thousand was to contest the action of an army approaching seventy thousand in strength. Sherman's mighty victories at Atlanta and his unlimited resources were automatic counters to any move that Hood might devise however bizarre its conception. Whatever the Yankee efforts, the "War Child" was to bear the brunt and carry the blame of failure.

On September 28th, 1864 Hood crossed the Chattahoochee at Pumpkintown and launched the Army of Tennessee on their "March to Oblivion." At the same time, Wheeler collected his force and moved south of Atlanta to annoy and watch Sherman in case he attempted to follow the main Confederate Army moving northward on his line of communications.

By October 12th Hood was at Resaca, the starting place of the campaigns of the previous summer. Sherman had risen to the bait and was following the northward marching Rebels. By the time Hood moved westward into north Alabama, Sherman was aware that it was unnecessary to pursue him further with his main army. He detached General George H. Thomas and his Army of the Cumberland plus other troops and sent them on to Nashville to deal with Hood. With his main force behind him, Sherman returned to Atlanta and his original purpose of laying waste central Georgia. Sherman's plan was a simple one. He would leave Atlanta behind him, burned to the ground and march to the sea at Savannah. Here he would be back on sea communications with the Federal Navy where re-supply would be no problem. Once this object was gained, he would then march northward through the Carolinas and join Grant before Petersburg. While on this march, Sherman programmed to turn the countryside into a barren wasteland thus finishing by starvation the work already begun on the battlefields.

On November 15th, 1864 Sherman started for the sea. Atlanta was destroyed even though it had no military value whatever, a grim portent of things to come. The Federal right wing consisted of the Fifteenth and Seventeenth Corps under Major General O. O. Howard and his left wing the Fourteenth and Twentieth Corps under Major General Henry W. Slocum. Slocum's Command was to move eastward toward Macon. A new wrinkle on warfare had been devised by Sherman to feed his army while on the march. A system of so-called "bummers" would be detailed from each division to move out into the countryside on each side of the marching columns, procure food and forage and return in the late evening with the loaded wagons. This system was to build the fantastic stories of pillage, rape, murder and arson that will be told for a thousand generations. Without discipline or control and with a license to commit any crime, however heinous, as long as they returned with the loaded wagons, the "bummers" made full use of this liberty. By the end of the first two weeks march, the Rebel cavalrymen showed them no mercy and the "bummers" expected none.

Wheeler's little band was at Lovejoy's Station when Sherman cut loose from Atlanta. He promptly moved over to the Macon Road and assaulted the head of the massive blue force crawling over the landscape. He could only annoy—he couldn't stop the forward momentum of the Federals. On the 16th General G. W. Smith in command of a rag-tag force of Georgia Homeguards numbering less than three thousand entrenched at Griffith. At sunset the gray riders retreated into Smith's trenches. Quickly dismounting the Command, Wheeler joined Smith in repelling several attacks, none of which was seriously pressed. At midnight Wheeler's scouts reported that a heavy Yankee force had passed through McDonough and was in the rear of Griffin. Quickly remounting the command, Wheeler rode rapidly for Macon by way of Forsythe.

General C. C. Crews' Brigade was sent to the Milledgeville Road and Breckenridge's Kentuckians to Griswoldville and the balance of the command hammered on to Macon. On arriving at this place Wheeler learned that General Hardee had been placed in command of the department and was frantically trying to put together a force to oppose the wrecking crews of Sherman. It was apparent to both men that it was a hopeless task. The little force of state troops under Smith and the cavalry under Wheeler was all there was—nothing else was forthcoming. At midnight the faithful scouts reported that Yankees were pouring down the roads from Hillsboro to Clinton—Wheeler moved to intercept.

With Harrison's Brigade in front followed by Dibrell and Ashby, the command moved out before daylight through an impenetrable fog. Wheeler, riding with his escort, was first into Clinton and rode squarely into Osterhaus' Corps moving through the town. It was too late to run when the discovery was made in the fog that he was in the midst of the Federals. Wheeler did the usual—he charged. Osterhaus' servants and several of his camp staff were captured before the surprised Yankees recovered their wits. A regiment of cavalry now charged Wheeler's little band and drove them at full speed from the town. At the outskirts, the Third Arkansas and Eighth Texas charged into the fray and sent the Federals reeling back into the town. The Federals promptly counter-charged with a full brigade, driving the Arkansans and Texans back into the countryside. Here, Dibrell and Ashby coming up at a gallop piled in and once again reversed the direction of flight. This time they collided with massive forces of blue infantry and drew off. The Federal horsemen captured in the fray were under the command of General Judson Kilpatrick, another throwoff from Grant's Army in Virginia.

Once again the scouts rode in with reports. This time their information was that Wood's Federal Division was moving rapidly eastward on the road to Griswoldville and Gordon. Warning Smith at Gordon that Wood was coming through, Wheeler moved over to the Griswoldville Road. By the time the circuitous ride was made, the Georgia Militia was already in action. Quickly dismounting Harrison's and Hagan's Brigades, Wheeler entered the trenches with the infantry. It was a short, nasty action. The highly trained, thoroughly motivated Federals smashed the Georgia boys in a series of vicious attacks. Several cavalrymen were killed desperately defending the lines while the militia made their escape. The Georgia State troops fought no more in the campaign.

Remounting the command, Wheeler swung wide around the Federal column and charged into Griswoldville breaking into the Yankee rear area. In the running fights that followed, sixty Yankees were captured and another twenty killed. Wheeler drew off without loss. By now it was apparent that it was a hopeless task to defend the state against Sherman. His columns were from fifteen to forty miles apart, moving on parallel lines, smashing, burning, and pillaging. Wheeler collected his force and retreated to Station Number 13, swimming the ice-cold Oconee River on the 24th. On the 25th the command was shifted to Sandersville, a position squarely in the middle of Sherman's three-pronged marching order.

Georgia was feeling the heel. In every town and hamlet, the Federals entered homes; ripped open bureaus with bayonets; slashed mattresses with knives and scattered feathers over the landscape; threatened inhabitants and guffawed with laughter when pleaded with not to destroy family heirlooms. The First Alabama Cavalry, a Federal unit made up of scallawags from north Alabama, were so murderous and destructive that even General Francis Blair, who held no compassion for Georgia, threatened to shoot the entire regiment for crimes against civilians. One bummer shot by a Kentucky man of Breckenridge's Brigade had thirty-three gold rings in his pocket. Another lot of twelve Federals captured by Crews' men and imprisoned in a private home in Gordon were forcibly taken from the guards by the Kentuckians and unceremoniously shot. They had stripped and beaten an old woman in an attempt to make her tell where she had hidden the family silver—the Kentuckians had exacted from them the full price of the crime. At night the horizon was lit up for miles by the towns and plantations burning to the ground. The war had taken a new turn and degenerated into a murderous onslaught on the civilian populace. The behavior of the Federals was rather well summed up in the same General Blair who, while using a plantation home as his headquarters and wishing to give an order to an officer in the yard, simply kicked out the front window to attract his attention.

After taking and sacking Milledgeville, the Fourteenth and Twentieth Corps moved on in the direction of Sandersville. Kilpatrick moved in the advance with the cavalry. Striking the main road some ten miles from the town, Kilpatrick ran into Crews' Brigade and chased them full tilt for some three miles. Here the old faithfuls showed up—Harrison, Ashby and Dibrell. With Wheeler in front the Arkansans and Texans came howling down on the Federals and the tide was reversed. With four Confederate Brigades crowding for space on the narrow road, firing point-blank with six shooters, the Federals were broken. For five miles the horse race went on until the hammering Federal horsemen reached safety behind the blue infantry. Some thirty Federals were killed or wounded in the fray.

The next day the gray horsemen fighting and retreating passed through Sandersville and gave it up to the Federal infantry. The town was promptly sacked and burned. At sunset Crews' scouts reported that a heavy force of enemy cavalry had crossed the Ogeechee at the shoals and were moving toward Augusta. Wheeler, knowing the immense value of the mills at Augusta, started immediately in pursuit. Leaving behind Iverson's Division to watch the Federal infantry, Wheeler moved on with Humes' and Allen's Divisions. Past Fenn's Bridge and on to Sylvan Creek the tired command rode through the night. At midnight the

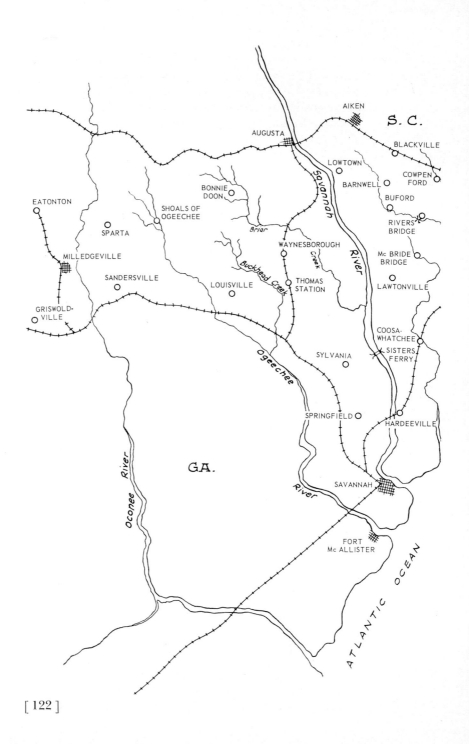

AIKEN

S. C.

AUGUSTA

BLACKVILLE

LOWTOWN

COWPEN
FORD

BARNWELL

BONNIE
DOON

BUFORD

EATONTON

SHOALS OF
OGEECHEE

RIVERS'
BRIDGE

SPARTA

Briar

WAYNESBOROUGH

Mc BRIDE
BRIDGE

MILLEDGEVILLE

Creek

SANDERSVILLE

Buckhead Creek

THOMAS
STATION

LAWTONVILLE

LOUISVILLE

Savannah

River

GRISWOLD-
VILLE

COOSA-
WHATCHEE

Ogeechee

SYLVANIA

SISTERS'
FERRY

SPRINGFIELD

HARDEEVILLE

GA.

River

SAVANNAH

Oconee River

FORT
Mc ALLISTER

ATLANTIC OCEAN

shadowy column entered the main Augusta Road at Reedy Creek. Here the Federal campfires burned in great profusion. Pushing Ashby's and Dibrell's Brigades ahead to attack the camps, Wheeler sent Harrison with Allen's Division to flank the escaping quarry on the north. The night silence was split with the roar of hooves, wild screeching yells and staccato crash of pistol shots. In the stampede that followed, Kilpatrick and most of his command escaped southward in the darkness leaving behind large numbers of prisoners and property. The camps were put to the torch and Wheeler pressed on in pursuit of the Federals.

At Bonnie Doon, Allen charged into the Federal rearguard causing them to halt and form line of battle. Wheeler now brought up Humes' Division and the whole command went in. The fighting drifted southward where Kilpatrick struck the Waynesborough road and escaped. The now totally exhausted Rebels fell from their saddles for a desperately needed rest for both horse and man. Augusta was saved but Waynesborough was now in the way. At 9 a. m. Wheeler had the troops back in the saddle and pushing southward. The entire day was spent extinguishing fires in dwellings and barns that had been fired along the route by the Federals. It was dark on the 26th when the head of the Rebel column rode into the furiously burning town of Waynesborough. The Federal rearguard was driven from the place and the rest of the night was spent putting out the fires and saving what was left of the town.

At 3 a. m. Wheeler moved to the attack. Humes' Division moved around the Federal right while Allen rode to attack him in front. Allen's fight was well underway when Humes with his division in line charged into the Federal flank. The hastily constructed trenches proved to be a death trap for Kilpatrick's dismounted men. The Rebels rode up and over them and the fighting was close and murderous. For some reason the Yankees refused to surrender and the Rebels killed them in wholesale lots. The mounted force fled in full retreat with Harrison and Dibrell pounding at their heels until refuge was sought behind Buckhead creek. The rear element didn't make it. The Eighth Texas, Eleventh Texas and Third Arkansas came up with them while they were in the process of crossing a swamp and charged in among them. Men were grabbed by their jacket fronts and shot with pistols jammed against their ribs. The infuriated Confederates fought like mad men, slashing and shooting their way through the mass of panicked blue coats in the narrow roads. When the bloody melee was ended some two hundred Federals were down to fight no more.

The remnant of Kilpatrick's command made their way across the swamp and holed up behind Buckhead Creek. The rickety bridge was fired by the rearguard just as Harrison rode up with the Eighth Texas. The Texans soon had the fire out and a handful of brave souls dashed across and took position on the opposite bank. As soon as this unit brought fire on the Federals, Colonel Henderson led the Third Arkansas across and drove in the main picket line. Wheeler now crossed with the main force and moved on in pursuit. Two miles from the bridge the Federals again appeared. This time they dug in on a line nearly a mile long in heavy timber. Darkness was now rapidly coming on and Wheeler was anxious to settle the issue. Rapidly forming the Third Arkansas in line and the Eighth and Eleventh Texas in column, forming a "T," he ordered the charge.

In General Wheeler's own words he said, "Nothing could have exceeded the gallantry with which these troops responded to the bugle's call and hurled themselves upon the enemy." As the Arkansans smashed the forward line in full charge, the Texans poured through the hole and got among the held horses. The Federal panic in the half-light was complete and final. The wild horse races over the fields and down the narrow lanes set off winking flashes of pistol fire in the darkness that continued all the way into Birdsville where the scattered Federals found safety behind the infantry. Kilpatrick did not again leave the protection of the marching infantry during the balance of the campaign.

Sherman's columns crawling over the land moved on through Louisville and Millen and on to Savannah. Wheeler's little command were mosquitoes after a giant. The Rebel horsemen could only scatter the bummers and shoot the plunderers, they could do nothing to retard the progress of this destructive juggernaut. On December 21st, 1864, Sherman rode down the streets of Savannah closing a campaign that would rage in the halls of controversy for the next thousand years.

On December 10th Wheeler took his command across the Savannah River at Sisters Ferry and moved southward on the South Carolina side to near Hardeeville. Here he received orders to picket the roads leading into South Carolina from Savannah thus opening the last phase of the last campaign of the Civil War.

The campaign from Atlanta to the sea was a hard one for Wheeler's men. They were entirely without wagons and had to forage from horseback. They had no cooking utensils and no way to prepare food except to wrap raw dough around ramrods and cook it on open fires. Some men plastered the dough on flat rocks and propped it near the fires to make a "corn pone." They had not been paid in a year and had had no clothing issued in sixteen months. The company commanders noted in the muster rolls that the men were ragged and cold but were fairly well fed. The cause for which they had fought so long and so well was doomed, but still they held on praying for some miracle that most knew would not be forthcoming. They had compiled an impressive record against Sherman's Army. They had captured three thousand cavalry horses and equipment; twelve hundred mules; two thousand head of beef cattle; four pieces of artillery with caissons and battery wagons; captured, killed or wounded more Federals than Wheeler had in his command and captured four thousand stand of small arms.

In early January, 1865, Lieutenant General Daniel H. Hill was appointed to Chief of Cavalry in South Carolina. This was a rare case of poor judgment on the part of President Davis since Hill was famed in the Confederacy for his hatred and contempt for the mounted arm. His first act was to write direct to General Iverson, by-passing Wheeler, with a vicious attack on Wheeler's Corps. He ordered Iverson to shoot on the spot what Hill termed, "Wheeler's marauders who were preying on the countryside." He said he had had many and bitter complaints against Wheeler's men for indiscriminate foraging and looting, a charge that was to rebound in a series of letters written direct to Davis by the division and brigade commanders in Wheeler's command denying the charges and voicing absolute confidence in the "War Child." Hill didn't maintain his command very long. In late January, General Wade Hampton, the Beau Sabreur of South Carolina, was sent by Lee to take command of the Rebel horsemen. He brought with him the crack brigade of General Matthew Calbraith Butler, a veteran of the Virginia campaigns.

With the coming of the last week of January in 1865, the Confederacy was wobbling on its last legs. General John Hood had marched his army from Atlanta into central Tennessee and destroyed it at Franklin and Nashville. The few survivors of this disaster had escaped into the country below the Tennessee River and Hood had resigned from the army. At Petersburg, Lee's fast dwindling army was starving to death in the trenches and facing an army three times their size. They were waiting for spring to

General Wade Hampton

Brig. General R. H. Anderson

Brig. General Felix Robertson

Maj. General
Judson Kilpatrick U.S.A.

come knowing that when it came, the end would not be far behind.

In Savannah, General William T. Sherman was briefing his commanders on the campaign just opening that was to seal the doom of the short-lived Confederate States of America. The right wing was to move from Hilton Head to Beaufort and up the Salkehatchie River aiming for Branchville. The left wing was to move up the west bank of the Savannah River; cross at Sisters Ferry; move toward Barnwell and Aiken and lay waste the countryside as they traveled.

By the last day of January the Yankees were well into South Carolina. Pocotaligo and Lawtonville were in their hands despite a countryside that was almost entirely under water. Humes' Division was assigned to picket the roads from Rivers Bridge on the Salkehatchie to Buford some fifteen miles upstream. It was here that the understrength Confederates met the main Federal effort. Rapidly corduroying the swamps and wading waste deep through the mire, the Federals assailed the Rebel lines at Rivers Bridge. The Third Arkansas and Eighth Tennessee were put into the trenches with the infantry while the Eighth and Eleventh Texas were kept mounted near Buford. The fighting in the dense woods and along the causeways was close and murderous for such few numbers. The bridge was held but General Mower got his Federals across near Buford and moved down on the Confederate right flank. The Texans charged them repeatedly but could not deter their forward progress. At Rivers Bridge the Arkansans backed out of the trenches and fought their way to their horses while the Georgia Infantry covered their retreat. In this action they lost Lieutenant Colonel Henderson who was severely wounded in the trench fighting. Major Blackwell was slightly wounded putting him out of action for a month. Several men were killed in the fracas from both the Arkansas and Tennessee Regiments.

Wheeler ordered Harrison's Brigade to move to the bridges and causeways at Cowpen Fords, burn these structures and then retire to Graham's Station on the South Carolina Railroad. Allen's Division was sent to Windsor and Johnston's Turnout. The balance of Humes' and Iverson's Divisions was dispersed along the invasion route of Sherman between Lowtown and Williston. The Federals were certainly making South Carolina feel the heel as Sherman had promised. Erwinton, Barnwell and Tredaway were burned to the ground. Burning, pillaging and looting, Kilpatrick's Cavalry moved on toward Aiken followed by the infantry.

Wheeler shifted his forces up the railroad toward Aiken. On February 8th Crews' Brigade was assailed at Williston and driven back toward Aiken. Hagan and Anderson promptly moved to his support. By daylight on the 9th Wheeler had collected the troops under Humes and Iverson and, after riding wide around Johnston's Turnout, rode into Aiken. The available infantry in Aiken numbered less than two thousand and the entire Confederate force was less than five thousand. At daylight on the 11th, the Federals moved to the attack. The fighting had moved into the streets of the town before Wheeler could determine their line and depth. Shells whistled over the housetops battering down the upper walls of the buildings while bullets ricocheted off the streets.

At the freight depot, Wheeler put Humes' entire division in line mounted while Allen's men held the adjacent streets dismounted. As the advancing Federals reached York Street they began to crowd as a result of the murderous fire from Allen's troopers and Wheeler instantly saw the opportunity. Turning to Humes he said, "General Humes, have at em!"

Rising in the stirrups, Humes' voice bellowed above the sound of the gunfire, "CHARGE!"

Giving forth a wild screech of the Plains Indians, the Texas Rangers clapped spurs to their mounts and thundered up the streets. They struck the Second U. S. Cavalry full in front. The Third Arkansas, now under Captain David W. Bizzell, swung around the Baptist Church and with the Tennesseans hard on their heels, rode down the flanks of the U. S. Regulars. Pistols blazing and yelling like banshees they ploughed through the column and rode full tilt into the Fifth U. S. Regulars. The momentum of their charge probably saved their lives. The Federals were jammed back into a cross street where they lost their maneuverability between the buildings. At this moment, Ashby and Dibrell entered the fray from another side street taking the Federals in flank. This broke up the show. In wild disorder the Yankees broke for the open country with Humes' Division pounding at their heels. For seven miles down the Lowtown Road the Rebels shot and sabred the Federals out of their saddles. Kilpatrick's Command was saved again by the infantry. In the streets of Aiken three hundred and ten Federals were down to fight no more. In addition, another two hundred were taken prisoner in the town and in the adjacent countryside. In this fray the Third Arkansas lost Captain Armstead Burwell, the AAG, who was severely wounded. As a result of this defeat, Kilpatrick was not again to leave the protection of the infantry until the armies had moved on into North Carolina.

Sherman's columns crawled on over the land. Columbia was destroyed and the armies moved on to Winnsboro and Cheraw leaving behind them a desolate wasteland. In the meantime, General Joseph E. Johnston had been recalled from home and placed in command of the scattered forces of the Confederacy in North Carolina. He was at this time making Herculean efforts to concentrate his army to oppose Sherman. The weary cavalrymen were reduced to burning bridges and shooting looters—they could do no more. At Averysboro, Hardee tore into Sherman's column causing a few days of precious delay for Johnston. At Smithfield Depot, Johnston was concentrating his force.

As the Federals neared Fayetteville, North Carolina, Kilpatrick once again left the protection of the infantry. His force numbered some fifteen hundred men and two women. Judson Kilpatrick believed in traveling in style. He had mortified the women of Georgia by quartering his lady friends in their homes at night, making no bones about his relationship with them. Kilpatrick was no more than three hours on his barn burning mission when Wade Hampton was aware of it. Hampton soon had couriers tearing over the countryside delivering his summons to concentrate. By the early morning of March 8th, Hampton had Butler's, Humes' and Allen's Divisions with him and was following in Kilpatrick's footprints. Hampton had him outnumbered nearly three to one and was closing in for the kill. In Kilpatrick's report he claimed he was out to "cut off the Rebel Cavalry," a stupid statement when Hampton was behind him on the line of march.

At late evening on the 9th, Kilpatrick went into bivouac at the junction of the Yadkin and Morganton Roads on Nicholson Creek. After dark a long column of determined Rebels was hurrying down the Morganton Road. At midnight Hampton silently halted the column just short of the Federal Camp. He sent Wheeler with Humes' and Allen's Divisions to the right, filing through a dense woods in the dark to come into line behind Nicholson Creek. Butler's Division continued on in the darkness and faced right into line, ninety degrees to Wheeler's line. This position put the Rebels on two sides of Kilpatrick's sleeping men. At the first faint rays of dawn, Hampton ordered the charge.

Butler's Division rode howling down on the Federal camp firing their pistols into the faces of the terrified men. Kilpatrick bolted from a farmhouse where he and his "ladies" had spent the night and fled into a swamp. On Humes' front all was panic. The Arkansans and Texans charged down through the trees toward the Federal tents and fell full stride into an impassable swamp. The reconnaissance had been tragically faulty. The aroused Federals now grabbed their guns and fought back like cornered animals. The fear of no quarter for barn burners made heroes out of cowards. The Third Arkansas was mired in the swamp, horses floundering and plunging. The Federals poured a hot fire into them from dry ground on the opposite bank. General Harrison was shot from his saddle while trying to reverse the direction of his men to come out of the swamp. General Humes was badly wounded in the front line. Colonels Hannon and Hagan fell, severely wounded. Hagan's Alabama Brigade was nearly destroyed while floundering around in the mud. In the meanwhile Butler's Confederates were riding back and forth through the Federal camps banging away with carbines and pistols.

Wheeler's men were finally extricated from the swamp and moved around to Butler's side of the action. As each brigade appeared on the scene they charged into the fray. One extraordinarily brave Yankee, loaded and fired a cannon charged with canister alone and unsupported. One of Butler's officers finally reached the gun and shot the Federal with a pistol. Butler later commented that it was a pity to kill so brave a man. There were many hilt-to-hilt encounters where mounted Confederates and dismounted Federals fought it out until one was killed. There was no quarter asked and none given. At 9 a. m. a brigade of Federal infantry was seen coming at a double quick along the Morganton Road, so Hampton called off the action.

The Confederates lost some seventy-five men killed and fifty wounded and the Federals lost four hundred captured, two hundred killed and a hundred and fifty wounded. The battered and bloody Confederates rode on into Fayetteville where they left their wounded to be cared for by the townspeople. Kilpatrick never fought again as a separate unit.

On March 19th Johnston moved from Smithfield with his concentrated army and assailed Sherman at Bentonville, North Carolina. Hampton had stalled the Federal advance near this tiny village long enough for Johnston to come up. Here in central North Carolina, the remnants of the once mighty Army of Tennessee, combined with a few men from Lee, carried a magnificent fight reminiscent of days of old. Sherman's Fourteenth Corps was wrecked in the terrible charge of the half starved

Confederates, but the Twentieth Corps coming on the scene stalled the effort and blunted the will. Bentonville was the dying gasp of the Confederacy.

In the late afternoon of the 21st a brigade of Federals worked their way around the Rebel left and was within a half mile of the only bridge across a steep and fast running creek, the last route of escape for Johnston's Army, when Hampton discovered them. At hand he had only the Eighth Texas—the famous Terry's Texas Rangers and a small brigade of Georgia infantry. Moving quickly to the rear he encountered General Hardee who had also seen the danger. Hardee joined the column and was with them when Captain "Doc" Matthews, the last surviving senior officer of the Texans, ordered the charge. The gallant old Fourth Tennessee joined in the assault after it was under way. The Third Arkansas and Eleventh Texas were too far away to participate. In this, the last heavy cavalry charge of the war, a unique and tragic event occurred. General Hardee's only son, a sixteen year old boy, had run away from school and insisted on joining the Texas Rangers. His father reluctantly approved, and at Bentonville saw him killed before his eyes in his first charge.

The fierceness of the charge at Bentonville carried with it the seeds of success. The Federals gave way under the weight of the Texans and Tennesseans, and Johnston's Army escaped northward.

On April 10th news leaked into North Carolina that Lee had surrendered to Grant at Appomattox, Virginia. Johnston's Army was now alone. On the 11th Sherman marched from Goldsborough to Smithfield and Johnston moved on to Raleigh. On the 13th Sherman had cleared Raleigh and was moving on to Durham. During the night of the 14th Johnson called in his senior commanders to announce the futility of carrying on a war that was already lost and continuing to kill men who would die in vain. They agreed and on the 14th, Johnston sent to Sherman a request for an armistice in order to discuss surrender terms. On the 18th the two men met in a one room farmhouse near Durham, North Carolina and stilled the guns that had thundered from Bull Run to Bentonville. Here, too, Johnston was told by Sherman that President Lincoln had been assassinated, a staggering blow to the southerners.

On April 24th Sherman was notified that his agreement with Johnston had been cancelled by the Federal Government and he was ordered to re-open hostilities. This was not entertained, how-

Bennett's Farmhouse near Durham, N. C. where Johnston surrendered to Sherman

Major W. H. Blackwell
Of Perryville

ever, and on the 26th of April another agreement was reached under the same terms offered to Lee by Grant. The terms were accepted and the war was over.

In the Confederate camps a rumor circulated that since Lincoln had been assassinated, the Yankees were going to transport all of Johnston's Army to northern prisons. It was false, but it had its effect. Thousands of men departed the camps, scattering through the countryside attempting to escape. Many of the cavalrymen from Texas, Arkansas and Tennessee struck out for home. The Kentuckians attached themselves to President Jefferson Davis' entourage which was attempting to escape into central Georgia and Florida. The majority of the army stayed on and were paroled in accordance with the surrender terms and left for home with the Federals' blessings.

In the ranks of the Third Arkansas Cavalry two hundred and sixty-four men had survived. Colonel Anson W. Hobson had recovered from his wounds received at Franklin and had traveled across the South to rejoin his regiment in North Carolina, arriving just in time to surrender with Johnston's Staff. Lieutenant Colonel Marzaime Henderson was absent wounded and Major William H. Blackwell was in command and had signed the surrender paroles. Several men of the Third Arkansas were captured at various places in the central South while making their way toward Arkansas. Some were with General Wheeler, who was posing as a Confederate Lieutenant and was attempting to escape into Texas and Mexico. They were captured at Conyer's Station near Atlanta and Wheeler was sent to prison at Fort Delaware, an infamous sink hole in Chesapeake Bay. Some of the Arkansans were captured in a body at Athens, Georgia while attempting escape.

Four long years of sacrifice and death, suffering and courage were behind them with nothing to show for their efforts but defeat. They rode away from North Carolina with the words of the "War Child" ringing in their ears.

> "Headquarters Cavalry Corps
> "April 28, 1865.

"Gallant Comrades; You have fought your fight. Your task is done. During a four years' struggle for liberty you have exhibited courage, fortitude and devotion. You are the victors of more than 200 sternly contested fields. You have participated in more than a thousand conflicts of arms. You are heroes! Veterans! Patriots! The bones of your comrades mark battlefields upon the soil of Kentucky, Virginia, North Carolina, South Carolina, Georgia, Alabama and Mississippi. You have done all that human exertion could accomplish. In bidding you adieu, I desire to tender my thanks for your gallantry in battle, your fortitude under suffering and your devotion at all times to the holy cause you have done so much to maintain. I desire also to express my gratitude for the kind feelings you have seen fit to extend toward myself, and to invoke upon you the blessing of our Heavenly Father, to whom we must always look in the hour of distress. Brethren, in the cause of freedom, comrades in arms, I bid you farewell.

"Joseph Wheeler,

"Major General.

"Official:

  "Wm. E. Waites,

    "Assistant Adjutant General."

APPENDIX I

PAROLE LIST

The Third Arkansas Cavalry Regiment was paroled in the town of Chesterfield, South Carolina. Having been on patrol in that area for sometime, they were still in the vicinity of the North Carolina border at the time of the surrender. They were ordered to the nearest Federal Post for the purpose of executing the standard parole. Many members refused to stay to be paroled and had started for Arkansas. They were captured at various places and paroled.

AT CHESTERFIELD, SOUTH CAROLINA

Colonel Anson W. Hobson

Major William H. Blackwell

Capt. John H. Bartholomew
Capt. William J. Bass
Capt. David W. Bizzell
Capt. Henry M. Corden
Lt. W. M. Daniels
Capt. Jeremiah Dumas
Capt. Thomas Goodin
Lt. Josiah Hensley
Lt. F. A. Hobson
Capt. C. W. Leake
Lt. Lewis Noland
Lt. E. D. Shuford
Lt. J. J. Sumpter
Capt. John Tindle
Pvt. C. G. Ashley
Pvt. N. Adkins
Sgt. R. H. Baber
Pvt. A. F. Barnard
Pvt. J. M. Barnett

Pvt. J. M. Barratt
Pvt. D. H. Barret
Pvt. L. D. Bata
Pvt. J. M. Battenfield
Pvt. T. V. Battle
Pvt. T. H. Beasley
Pvt. Samuel Bell
Pvt. S. E. Benson
Pvt. G. W. Brazill
Pvt. A. J. Bridges
Pvt. William F. Brooks
Pvt. Joseph C. Bunker
Pvt. A. B. Burks
Pvt. William Burkes
Sgt. George R. Buster
Pvt. G. W. Campbell
Pvt. John Capps
Pvt. John H. Casteel
Pvt. S. Chambers

Pvt. John M. Chenault
Pvt. R. L. Cobb
Cpl. William H. Cobb
Pvt. R. A. Cochran
Pvt. G. W. Coppock
Pvt. J. N. Cowger
Pvt. A. H. Cross
Pvt. James F. Crowson
Pvt. John S. Davis
Pvt. Bryant Dees
Pvt. J. H. Dixon
1st Sgt. John T. Downs
Pvt. John T. Dunford
Pvt. G. W. Evans
1st Sgt. Robert Farrish
Sgt. A. W. Frazier
Pvt. A. J. Garrison
Pvt. Andrew Glasgow
Pvt. Zachariah Gray
Sgt. D. M. Green
Pvt. James S. Green
Pvt. B. B. Haigwood
Pvt. William Haltom
Pvt. Josua Harp
Pvt. W. B. Hawkins
Pvt. George Hecklar
Pvt. R. F. Hemphill
1st Sgt. J. P. Henderson
Pvt. P. N. Herrald
Sgt. J. E. Hillman
Pvt. S. J. Hillman
Pvt. John R. Hobbs
Pvt. D. H. Hood
Pvt. W. B. Howard
Cpl. E. M. Hunnicutt
Pvt. George Hunnicutt
Pvt. G. W. Ivey
Pvt. M. S. Ivey
Pvt. A. J. Jackson
Pvt. S. James
Pvt. F. S. Johnson
Pvt. Joseph Johnson
Pvt. George Kellam
Cpl. J. J. Kendrick
Bugler A. E. Kenneday
Pvt. E. Kilpatrick
Pvt. E. P. Kirksey
Pvt. C. J. Knight
Pvt. F. M. Lackey
Pvt. M. Lawrance
Pvt. John T. Leer

Pvt. J. P. Lennox
Pvt. Washington Lowe
Pvt. James B. Mangum
Pvt. M. W. Mason
Pvt. D. M. Mays
Pvt. James A. McCall
Pvt. Archie McClain
Pvt. W. B. McCraw
Pvt. I. H. McCullough
Pvt. Thomas A. McHenry
Sgt. John M. Moore
Pvt. R. M. Moore
Pvt. G. W. Moreland
Pvt. John Morrison
Pvt. A. A. Moss
Pvt. Marion Morse
Pvt. J. M. Mullins
Pvt. Isaac Myers
Pvt. D. H. Neeley
Sgt. J. O. Nicholson
Pvt. A. A. Obear
1st/Sgt. William T. Organ
Sgt. W. M. Owen
Pvt. J. T. Owens
Pvt. Tomas Owens
Pvt. A. Parks
Pvt. Josiah Patterson
Pvt. Samuel Patterson
Pvt. Thomas Payne
Pvt. N. B. Petty
Pvt. D. H. Pilkington
Pvt. Abraham Plunkett
Pvt. A. A. Porter
Pvt. William Pritchard
Pvt. Samuel Pursley
Pvt. Jeremiah Ragsdill
Pvt. J. E. Ratliffe
Pvt. M. L. Ray
Pvt. L. R. Redding
Pvt. Corrin Reid
Pvt. F. M. Robinson
Pvt. Ellsberry Roberts
Pvt. William T. Roberts
Cpl. H. W. Rodgers
Pvt. Ed Rucks
Pvt. Thomas C. Scott
Pvt. R. M. Scruggs
Pvt. Jackson Shipe
Pvt. J. W. Skief
Pvt. W. E. Smith
Pvt. J. L. Spikes

Sgt. D. W. Starbuck
Pvt. G. W. Stubblefield
Pvt. William S. Sutton
Pvt. William A. Sydnor
Cpl. John Thomas
Pvt. N. D. Thomas
Pvt. George H. Thompson
Pvt. G. W. Thompson
Pvt. R. M. Thompson
Sgt. W. B. Thompson
Pvt. William M. Ticer
Pvt. Joseph B. York
Pvt. James C. Trout
Pvt. R. M. Turner
Sgt. Robert N. Turner

Pvt. J. B. Tutton
Sgt. Calvin Tyler
Pvt. G. W. Vestal
Pvt. Frank Wallbrink
Pvt. Robert R. Wallace
Pvt. W. B. Walters
Pvt. C. P. Warren
Pvt. H. H. Weaver
Pvt. H. C. Weaver
Pvt. John C. Wells
Pvt. W. C. Wheeler
1st/Sgt. R. A. Wiley
Pvt. Joseph H. Wilkes
Sgt. Finch M. Winburne
Pvt. Jasper Wright

AT ATHENS, GEORGIA

Pvt. J. Aker
Sgt. Austin Bartlett
Pvt. William Beam
Pvt. J. E. Billiss
Pvt. J. Blakely
Pvt. A. W. Braggs
Pvt. J. T. Bromly
Pvt. G. M. Bryne
Pvt. J. E. Bullock
Pvt. R. Burd
Pvt. D. Carpenter
Pvt. B. Cleveland
Pvt. T. H. Coyler
Pvt. R. J. Delaway
Pvt. M. Durritt
Pvt. W. Ellis
Pvt. W. M. Grayman
Pvt. J .P. Hart
Sgt. H. P. Heard
Pvt. L. Hendrick
Pvt. B. Herden
Pvt. J. W. Holmes
Pvt. L. Hopper
Pvt. S. E. Howllery

Pvt. J. E. Hunter
Pvt. E. Joy
Pvt. B. A. Kerrey
Pvt. C. E. Lackman
Pvt. H. L. Leman
Pvt. J. C. Lindsig
Pvt. J. Lowrie
Pvt. J. W. Middleton
Pvt. S. Munn
Pvt. J. N. Organ
Pvt. J. E. Petts
Pvt. G. Price
Pvt. A. Roberts
Pvt. J. M. Rowmer
Pvt. H. Ruder
Pvt. E. Rudsil
Pvt. W. H. Says
Pvt. E. Stayker
Pvt. G. W. Watson
Pvt. G. H. West
Pvt. G. W. West
Pvt. A. J. Williams
Pvt. E. A. Wise

OTHERS

Lt. J. P. Bata—Memphis, Tennessee

Pvt. J. P. Battenfield—Nashville, Tennessee

Pvt. T. Birt—Memphis, Tennessee

Capt. Armstead Burwell—C. S. A. Hospital, Charlotte, North Carolina

Pvt. J. S. Callins—Columbus, Mississippi

Lt. J. Cannon—Thomasville, Georgia

Pvt. James W. Cowan—Memphis, Tennessee

Pvt. T. J. Culpepper—Talladega, Alabama

Pvt. Thomas E. Daily—Big Black River, Mississippi

Captain Robert H. Dedman—Charlotte, North Carolina

Pvt. J. P. Dye—Memphis, Tennessee

Pvt. James Gatee—Memphis, Tennessee

Pvt. James M. Gollaher—Talladega, Alabama

Capt. Oliver C. Gray—Ship Island, Mississippi

Sgt. W. P. Hale—Memphis, Tennessee

Sgt. Percival Henderson—Camp Douglas, Chicago, Illinois

Pvt. William Jackson—Jackson, Mississippi

Pvt. G. W. Jones—Fort Delaware Prison, Delaware

Pvt. J. R. Laurence—Memphis, Tennessee

Pvt. J. W. Lovejoy—Memphis, Tennessee

Pvt. C. S. Mason—Shreveport, Louisiana

Pvt. J. T. McCerred—Columbus, Mississippi

Sgt. A. D. McCullough—Meridian, Mississippi

Pvt. J. A. McGee—Memphis, Tennessee

Pvt. T. G. Measels—Memphis, Tennessee

Pvt. J. M. Merryman—Exchanged, Fort Smith, Arkansas

Pvt. S. H. Montgomery—Memphis, Tennessee

Pvt. W. H. Phillips—Camp Douglas, Chicago, Illinois

Pvt. W. B. Porter—Memphis, Tennessee

Pvt. Luther Powell—New Orleans, Louisiana

Pvt. E. R. Robbins—Montgomery, Alabama

Pvt. S. A. Sammons—Camp Winder, Richmond, Virginia

Pvt. G. W. Scott—Memphis, Tennessee

Pvt. A. J. Sliver—Meridian, Mississippi

Sgt. G. H. Stubblefield—Montgomery, Alabama

Pvt. P. Tollison—Memphis, Tennessee

Pvt. J. L. Vanhoozer—Memphis, Tennessee

Sgt. Tomas A. Wiley—Greensboro, North Carolina

Pvt. Harry Williamson—Shreveport, Louisiana

APPENDIX II

SELECTED BIBLIOGRAPHY

Arkansas History Commission, Confederate Collection, Little Rock

Barron, S. B., The Lone Star Defenders, Neale Co., (New York, 1908)

Battles and Leaders of the Civil War, Four Volumes (New York, 1888)

Bearss, Edwin C., Decision in Mississippi, (Jackson, 1962)

Civil War Times, Various Issues, (Gettysburg, Penna.)

Collier, Calvin L., First In—Last Out, (Little Rock, 1961)

Confederate Soldier in the Civil War, Pagent Books, (New Jersey, 1956)

Giles, L. B., Terry's Texas Rangers, Private Publication

Hood, John B., Advance and Retreat, (New Orleans, 1880)

Johnston, Joseph E., Narrative, (New York, 1874)

Jones, Katherine M., When Sherman Came, Bobbs-Merril, (New York, 1964)

National Archives, Confederate Collection, Washington D. C.

Oates, Stphehen B., Confederate Cavalry West of the River, University of Texas, (Austin, 1961)

Official Atlas, The Civil War, Praeger Books, (New York, 1958)

Photographic History of the Civil War, Ten Vol., (New York, 1912)

Southern Historical Society Papers, (Richmond, 1876-1930)

U. S. War Department: The War of the Rebellion, The Official Records, The Union and Confederate Armies. (Washington, D. C., 1876-1930)

West Point Atlas of American Wars, Praeger Books, (New York, 1959)